EX LIBRIS

ADRIENNE HERBERT

POWER HOUR

How to focus on your goals and
create a life you love

HUTCHINSON
BOOKS

1 3 5 7 9 10 8 6 4 2

Hutchinson
20 Vauxhall Bridge Road
London SW1V 2SA

Hutchinson is part of the Penguin Random House group of companies
whose addresses can be found at global.penguinrandomhouse.com

Copyright © Adrienne Herbert 2020

Adrienne Herbert has asserted her right under the
Copyright, Designs and Patents Act, 1988,
to be identified as the author of this work.

First published in the United Kingdom by Hutchinson in 2020

www.penguin.co.uk

A CIP catalogue record for this book is available from the British Library.

ISBN 9781786332691 (Hardcover)
ISBN 9781786332707 (Trade paperback)

Text design by Andreas Brooks

Typeset in 10.84/19 pt Source Serif Variable
by Integra Software Services Pvt. Ltd, Pondicherry

Printed and bound in Great Britain by Clays Ltd, Elcograf S.p.A.

The authorised representative in the EEA is Penguin Random House Ireland,
Morrison Chambers, 32 Nassau Street, Dublin D02 YH68.

Penguin Random House is committed to a sustainable future for
our business, our readers and our planet. This book is made from
Forest Stewardship Council® certified paper.

To anyone who knows
they can do more,
achieve more
and become more.

Contents

Introduction 1

The Power of Mindset 19

How to Create Powerful Habits 63

The Power of Movement 97

The Power of Sleep 133

The Power of People 171

The Power of Purpose 209

Create Your Own Power Hour 257

Acknowledgements 295

Endnotes 297

Introduction

Sometimes, it feels as though I've talked about nothing else but the Power Hour for the last few years. My morning Power Hour was born in January 2017, and I'll admit I am the kind of person who loves that new-year-new-start energy. I also love lists and I love making plans, so I always have a paper diary in which I write down my goals and aspirations for the year ahead. In January 2017, I found myself desperately in need of a new start. The previous year had been a tough one and I had reached that place where change is born out of necessity. When you're at an all-time low, it can feel overwhelming to think about your 'big life plan', especially when your life has swerved in a completely different direction to the one you had in mind. At that time, my vision and dream were to create and nurture a big family. My son, Jude, was five years old, and my husband and I had been trying to fall pregnant again since Jude's second birthday. My husband and I had always wanted to have children – right from the start we agreed we'd have at least three, maybe even four. So after almost three years of trying *everything*, I found myself feeling frustrated, angry and hopeless.

What do you do when it seems like nothing is going to plan? I believe that you must know when to start, when to continue and when to stop. Trust me when I say we'd done all we could, and eventually – after lots of discussions, research, doctor's appointments and tests – we decided that our best chance of having another baby would be IVF treatment. If you're reading this and you've never had IVF, I'm sure you've probably heard of it, and you might even have friends who have gone through it. And if you're reading this having gone through it yourself, then I salute you. You deserve a fucking medal. For me, IVF treatment proved that humans are capable of enduring just about anything when they're desperate. Perhaps I didn't see it at the time, but when I look back now, I realise that is exactly how I felt throughout the entire process – desperate. I was desperate for our son to have a sibling to grow up and make memories with. I was desperate to be part of the conversation at baby swimming with my mates who were expecting baby number two. I was desperate to have an answer whenever someone asked me when we were going to have another child. I was desperate to give my husband good news, instead of seeing the disappointment and heartbreak on his face every time I came out of the bathroom with another negative pregnancy test. For almost three years I prayed, I cried, I waited and I remained hopeful.

When we started IVF, I felt conflicted. (And not just because of the insane amount of hormones that you have to inject into your body on a daily basis throughout the treatment.) My head was telling me that this would definitely work; the specialists knew what they were doing after all, and I was young and healthy so there was no reason why it *wouldn't* work. I told myself that my mind would influence my body and so I *needed* to truly believe the treatment was going to work. To be honest, I don't think I would have been able to endure the physical and emotional challenges of the treatment if I hadn't had faith that it was going to be successful. I had to convince myself that it would all be worth it. I know many women who have had IVF treatment and

I think they would agree with me – it's the only way you can get through it. But, on the other hand, my heart was cautious and afraid. How would I cope if it didn't work? This felt like our last resort, and we knew we couldn't afford to pay for another round of treatment if it failed. I felt like my entire life's happiness was dependent on this.

To say it was an emotional rollercoaster would make it sound a lot more fun than it actually was, but after weeks of painful procedures and emotional torture, we finally left the fertility clinic with the good news. Yes, it had worked – I was pregnant! I remember every single minute of that car journey home. I was so excited, my mind racing to imagine the year ahead. I pictured myself with a big belly again, and I thought about telling Jude he would have a baby brother or sister. I wanted this for him just as much – if not more – than I wanted it for myself. I don't think you can compare the relationship you have with a sibling to anything else, and it's difficult for me to imagine my life without mine. And since I'd been daydreaming about this precise moment for the last three years, I already had a long list of potential names. I could pretty much imagine the baby's face. So with each day that passed, we began to relax and celebrate as we told our family and a handful of close friends. We decided we'd wait a few more weeks before telling Jude (five-year-olds are notoriously bad at keeping secrets and I knew he'd probably announce it to his whole class the first chance he got).

We never told Jude the news. Less than four weeks later, I was woken up by pain and stomach cramps. I knew something wasn't right, but I tried to ignore it and pretend everything was fine. My husband went to work, I took Jude to school and as I walked back home I prayed that the pain would go away. But by midday I was in agony and I could no longer ignore it. I knew what was happening: I was having a miscarriage. We'd waited so long for this baby, and in one afternoon, along with the joy and the hope, it was all gone. We all have to face painful experiences – sadly, no one is exempt from adversity, setbacks, failure, heartbreak, grief or loss. Some have to face a lot more than others and there is no justification for the amount of suffering some people endure in one lifetime. We each have a story, and this is just a small part of mine.

Even though I didn't know it then, this difficult time in my life would change everything. At that point, it felt like I couldn't have the one thing I wanted more than anything else – but I also knew I couldn't carry on relentlessly pursuing my dream of having more children, to the detriment of everything else in my life. My marriage, my finances, my friendships and most importantly my *outlook* were all being negatively impacted. I felt jealous of friends who were having babies, and I felt angry when they complained about the sleepless nights. I had a constant feeling of guilt that Jude was an only child. I couldn't understand how or why this was happening. What was the purpose? Was it supposed to teach me something? Hard as I looked, I couldn't find a silver lining – the disappointment was crushing, and I was heartbroken and angry at God. I felt incredibly grateful to have Jude and I was reminded of that every time I heard him call me 'Mummy', but that didn't take away the feeling of sadness underneath it all. When I looked ahead to the future, I could no longer envision the life I'd dreamed of. It's hard to see the light at the end of the tunnel when you're lying face down on the ground. Back then my mind was fixed and I believed that any alternative future would only ever be second best.

That was, until two very important things happened. The first was an opportunity that came at just the right time; the second was my willingness to take it.

At the start of 2017, I got a call from Paul Brady, the PR Manager at Adidas UK, whom I'd worked with before. He told me that Adidas had a few race places in London's iconic marathon, and he asked if I'd like to run the race as a member of the 'AR' running community. It was January, the April marathon was just 14 weeks away, and I'd never even run more than 10K. So *of course* the rational response was: 'Oh my gosh, yes! I've never run a marathon before, but yes! Count me in!' As I hung up the phone, I was buzzing with excitement. But that rush was soon pushed aside by the onset of self-doubt. *Are you kidding? You can't run 26 miles!* it chided me. *You're not a marathon runner. You're a mum and a fitness trainer. You don't even know how to train for a marathon. Surely you'll need a coach? Only real runners take on marathons. There must be lots of other runners who would love to do this iconic race, you should give the place to one of them. Do you even have time for this right now? It's January, it's freezing outside. You're a fair-weather runner, Adrienne. Call him back and tell him you've changed your mind.* After a few minutes of initial panic, I composed myself and spent the next couple of hours looking at marathon training plans online and reading articles about how to prepare for your first marathon. I hadn't realised till then how much I *needed* this focus – how essential it was for me to channel my mental and physical energy into something totally new. I'd spent the last few years tracking my cycle and calculating when I would be ovulating each month. I'd poured hours into analysing the stats and data about fertility-boosting diets and how to optimise sperm motility. If I could bring that same dedication and commitment to training for this race, then maybe running my first marathon wasn't such a crazy idea.

But there was the question of time – training for a marathon demands an increasing number of hours each week as you prepare your body. As well as the actual running time, you have to make time for recovery, stretch, see a physiotherapist and do strength-training exercises and drills to improve your technique and prevent injuries. How was I going to find all those extra hours? Together with my family-life commitments, I was coaching eight clients each week in one-to-one personal training sessions. I was writing weekly blog posts as well as the occasional article for health and wellness magazines, and I'd started partnering with brands to create social media campaigns. Come the end of the day, once Jude was in bed and I had eaten dinner, the thought of heading out in the cold for a 60-minute training run was unappealing, to say the least. That's when the realisation hit me: if I wanted to find an extra hour each day to train for this race, the simple solution was to get up an hour earlier instead.

Jude would typically wake up around 6:30am, meaning I'd need to head out at 5:30am. If just the thought of this repulses you, then please bear with me. Trust me, I wasn't exactly thrilled by the idea either at first. (Have I mentioned it was January?) But I had to find a way to prepare for this race, so I thought I'd just give it a go. (One thing you'll learn about me as you read this book is that when I say 'give it a go', what I actually mean is: I will give it absolutely everything I've got; I'll obsess over every single detail and I'll either succeed or die trying. *That* is my definition of 'give it a go'.) When I'd said yes to Paul on the phone, I'd been naive about what I was signing up for – but deep down, I also knew that no matter how hard it was going to be, I would find a way to make it happen. I wanted a new challenge, one where I was in control of the outcome.

*

Throughout this book, I'll tell you what happened in the months and years that followed, as a result of this extra hour in the morning. At that moment, I had no idea that winding the clock back by an hour would change just about everything – from my relationships, to my career, to what I fundamentally believed to be possible for my life. I've used that extra hour to read more, listen to podcasts, complete online courses, train for marathons, stretch, meditate, journal and even write this book. The Power Hour is not about getting up at 5:00am, it's not about being crazy productive or about running five miles every day before breakfast. Truth be told, as long as it's the first hour, I don't care what time you choose to get up each day – the time itself is irrelevant. The Power Hour is a mindset; it's about empowering yourself to make a choice and take action. It's a way for you to focus on your goals and create a life that you love. Pre-Power

Hour (as I now think of it), I wasn't able to even imagine the life I live today. I had no idea about what was possible because I never took the time to find out.

I can honestly say that the Power Hour has had an immeasurable impact on my life. Today, I work in the wellness industry as a coach and brand consultant, motivational speaker and podcast host. I have completed road races in more than 14 countries and delivered talks to the employees of some of the world's biggest organisations, including Apple, ASOS and Barclays. I've hosted more than 100 interviews on the Power Hour podcast. I work with industry leaders, business founders, Olympic athletes, psychologists, innovators and change makers to learn more about their daily habits and their rules to live by, and to find out what motivates them to get out of bed each day. I have learned so much from collaborating with high-performing people and, as a result, I have identified common attributes and key principles that many of them share. In this book, I will highlight the main areas to focus on if you want to unlock your full potential and achieve both personal and professional success.

Now, you might not want to run a marathon or start a company or write a book, but I guarantee there is *something* that you want to achieve. It doesn't matter how big or small it might seem to others – the Power Hour is about *you* and *your* goals. We have all read books that tell you to simply find your purpose and follow your passion. But in today's super-charged, fast-paced world, that advice is easier said than done. The modern world is complex, and we are overwhelmed with choices, ideas, new trends and noise, from the moment we wake up in the morning until we go to sleep at night. Many people feel as though they are simply trying to keep up. Sure, maybe one day you'll follow your passion, but right now? You just don't have the time. How many times have you said, 'I'd love to do that, but I don't have time,' or 'One day, I'm going to start that project, maybe when I have more money, or when my kids are older'? I get comments like these a lot from friends and clients – *and* I used to say them myself.

Your time has never been more valuable: it is the only thing you can't buy more of. Now, I'm not suggesting every hour of every day should be 'productive' – in fact, quite the opposite. You just need to start with *one.* By taking only one hour at the start of each day to do something – anything – that you choose, you are making a decision to reclaim your time, and your power. Throughout the day there will be a growing number of things simultaneously competing for your attention: emails, WhatsApp messages, work deadlines, kids, errands. So, before the rest of the world is awake, before you start to give your time and your energy away, start your day by dedicating one hour to yourself, to creating a life you truly love and to becoming the person you want to be.

From the importance of daily movement, to the science of creating new habits, to developing a growth mindset and boosting self-confidence, this book will give you the tools and the processes I have learned so you can create a routine that works for you. I want you to read this book and feel motivated to make a change in your life, big or small, but I'll warn you now that the feeling of motivation is not going to be enough. You will need to take action! Think of this book as a manual, a blueprint and a toolkit. You don't read a driving manual and then sit in the back and let someone else steer the car – you take the wheel for yourself. If you're inspired by some of the suggestions in this book, give them a go. But remember that they are simply suggestions – there is no foolproof recipe for success. (I'm sorry to say that if you skip to the back, you won't find a cheat sheet or a page of answers.) I hope that you'll discover things in this book that you've perhaps never thought about before. I also expect that there may be parts which you do not agree with or that do not resonate with you. And that's okay. I'd love for these words to start a conversation. Throughout this book you'll find conversations I've had with others, people whom I respect and admire – each for different reasons – and who have taught me a lot. I hope that I have done justice to them all, and that you can learn something from their words of wisdom too.

Each chapter can be read alone and in any order, so if you want to head straight to the Power of Movement or you want to start off with the Power of Sleep, go ahead – just make sure you have a pencil ready to underline the parts you want to come back to or share with someone else. This is not a library book – it does not need to stay pristine. I want this book to be carried around in your bag, with some pages stained by coffee and covered in food crumbs, the bottom corner crinkly because you accidentally dipped it in the bathwater, and full of receipts that you've used as temporary bookmarks along the way. I would be honoured if it were to be passed on to someone else once you've finished. I did not write this book for it to look nice on a coffee table or to brighten up your shelf next to that cactus plant. I hope that it will be impactful, and that you will come back to it again and again when you need a dose of inspiration and encouragement.

So, are you ready for your initiation into the official Power Hour crew? Place one hand on your heart and repeat after me: 'I shall not hit snooze. EVER.' There's a reason why I distrust the snooze button so deeply. Imagine that you're waiting for a bus, which runs every ten minutes and is going to take you to *insert place you love here* (think Disneyland, Coachella, a sample sale at Gucci . . .). When the first bus comes, do you let it pass and just think, *Oh it's fine, I'll get the next one or maybe the one after that*? No – you jump on that first bus because you're excited to get going! Similarly, on a Monday morning when your alarm goes off and you hit snooze, you're telling yourself that you're not excited to get going. That whatever you've got to do that day is something you'd rather put off. You don't want to face it, at least not for another 10 or 20 minutes. If this is indeed the case for you, then you need to find ways to add more joy to your day. I'm not saying that I wake up every morning as if I'm going to Disneyland, but I do wake up with a sense of urgency. There is joy in every single day of my life because I've created a life that I love, and because I choose to look out for those 'good' things. They can be big or small but I know that they're there. I look at my schedule written out in my paper diary and I can't wait to get to it. That's why the first hour is so critical to the rest of the day. It sets the tone for what comes next.

Once you discover the life-changing benefits of the Power Hour, get ready to talk about it with anyone and everyone. People will ask you, 'Why?' Why would you *willingly* get out of bed an hour earlier? But do not be put off as they scoff and attempt to convince you that you're mad – after all, '*No great mind has ever existed without a touch of madness.*' (Thanks, Aristotle.) Trust me, after a few months, their *why* will be replaced with *how*. When we discover something that sparks change, other people will notice it too.

Before you dive in, I'd like to add this – if you take only one thing away from this book, let it be that it is possible to change and transform your life. You owe it to yourself to pursue a life that you truly love. If you don't know where to start, start with just one hour each day. The first hour. The Power Hour.

You can do hard things.

The Power of Mindset

As someone who has faced many challenges throughout their life, I've always been curious to understand
why some people sink and others swim in the face of
adversity. Why do some react to failure by becoming
even more driven to succeed, while others become
paralysed by the fear of failing again? What determines
our outlook and shapes our mindset? There will always
be two sides to every coin, a list of pros and cons for
any unique situation, a positive and negative version
of the same story. And the simple answer is, it's up
to you to choose to focus on the side that will benefit
you the most, and develop what is known as a 'growth
mindset'.

The terms 'fixed mindset' and 'growth mindset' were
coined by the scientist Dr Carol Dweck in her seminal
book, *Mindset: Changing the way you think to fulfil your
potential*. Dweck explains that having a fixed mindset

means you believe that your character, skills and creative abilities are fixed. You can only do so much with the cards that life has dealt you; in other words, unless you were born with an exceptional gift or talent, there is a cap on what you can achieve because your genetics will ultimately determine your success. On the other hand, having a growth mindset means that you believe you can continually develop your abilities and learn new skills. You do not allow failure to discourage you; instead, you view failure as an opportunity to learn and improve. Developing a growth mindset will help you to achieve just about anything.

As Dweck argues, 'It is not just our abilities and talent that bring us success – but whether we approach our goals with a fixed or growth mindset. With the right mindset, we can motivate our children to raise their grades, as well as reaching our own goals – both personal and professional.' A growth mindset will help you find solutions to the inevitable problems and challenges that life brings, and it will empower you to learn from mistakes instead of repeating them. Cultivating a growth mindset is critical if you want to be able to thrive under pressure, take risks and accept that failure is just a part of the story. It will allow you to take ownership of your own life and to seek the experiences, opportunities and people that will support you in the pursuit of your goals. What you do and what you say will reinforce your mindset every single day. This will ultimately determine what other people expect from you and, most importantly, what you expect from yourself.

*

I remember reading *Mindset* for the first time, roughly four years ago on a flight home from Paris. I was travelling alone and, when I turned the final page, I just felt frustrated that I had no one to share that exciting lightbulb moment with. (The guy sitting next to me was asleep, and I don't think he would have appreciated me waking him up to discuss the concept of creating an empowering mindset.) The book challenged me to think about my career path, my relationships and the way I parent my son. It made me reflect on my own attitude to life, and the way my mindset had developed as a child.

While growing up, I always felt like I could do pretty much anything. Maybe my innate confidence in my own capabilities was due to having younger siblings and taking on responsibility at a young age, or perhaps I'm just wired that way. I see time and time again that children are far more curious than adults, and they ask more questions in an attempt to explore the world and push boundaries. In our early years, we are far more open-minded and don't place limits on ourselves or our imagination. Through play and pretend, we transform everyday objects into something else entirely: a stick easily becomes a sword; a cardboard box transforms into a house and then a race car; a bed sheet is our hidden den; and the sofa turns into a balance beam. We envision and enact becoming an astronaut or a deep-sea diver. My son loves the Avengers and superhero stories, and so we've spent hours reading Marvel books and comics together. I always tell him that, even if we can't be superheroes, we can still be superhumans: our ability to imagine is one of our superpowers.

Our conscious imagination could be our greatest evolutionary advantage compared to other species. In his book *The Gap: The Science of What Separates Us from Other Animals*, psychologist Thomas Suddendorf provides the first definitive account of what makes human minds different to those of other animals, and how this difference arose. He explains that two innovations are responsible for the ways in which our minds appear so distinct: our open-ended ability to imagine and reflect on different situations; and our insatiable drive to connect with others, to link our minds together. Having a conscious imagination gives us the ability to dream, to play pretend and to visualise a whole new reality. Mind coach Natalie Pennicotte-Collier calls this 'the theatre of our minds'. She teaches visualisation exercises to some of the world's most elite sportsmen and women, including Formula One drivers and Team GB Paralympic athletes. 'Seeing is believing, but if you can't see it *yet*, close your eyes and visualise it,' she told me.

This 'superpower', however, usually diminishes as we grow up, learn more about the world and become acutely aware of the gap between reality and fantasy. For most people, this means they start focusing less on *what if* and more on *how to*. We are taught to curb our enthusiasm; and sadly, for many, once they are grown up their dreams stay dreams.

As a child, if I didn't know how to do something, I'd try to figure it out, often through trial and error (and often by myself). I taught myself to ride a bike, plait my hair, cook dinner, and I even learned how to change a fuse in a plug when the washing machine stopped working. Perhaps this was the result of growing up without a 'man of the house'. My mum worked hard and I believe she did her best, but one parent can't always do the job of two. There were no YouTube tutorials in the '90s and we didn't have access to the internet at home until I was 13, but as we've all heard, where there's a will, there's a way. Then technology made everything a little easier. Back in 2012, when I started blogging, I learned how to build a website using a basic blog template by watching video tutorials on YouTube. When I first started my personal training business, I had no idea what I was doing. I didn't know how much to spend on advertising, how to manage costs or how to do a tax return, so I asked an accountant to explain it to me. When I wanted to reach more people than the 20 clients I had in front of me, I learned how to film, edit and upload workout videos online. (This was about five years before video editing apps, GIF makers and TikTok.) In hindsight, I think I probably developed a growth mindset out of necessity, and have been unknowingly practising positive thinking techniques for as long as I can remember – long before encountering Dr Dweck and her book. But what *Mindset* did for me was provide confirmation that my mentality growing up impacted my ability to excel later in life, and it taught me that anyone can change and develop their mindset through thoughtful action and repetition.

I have had the privilege of speaking to a number of incredible people about their mindset, from Manchester United football player Chris Smalling, to international DJ and broadcaster Trevor Nelson, to business pioneers such as Jacqueline Gold and Ben Branson. Of course, there is some disparity from person to person – not least because of their individual personality, upbringing and chosen industry – but one thing that all of these high-performing people consistently demonstrate is a growth mindset. I spoke to Lena Kessler, a sports psychologist and performance consultant, about this common attribute. She works with elite youth athletes in a variety of sports, including boxing, figure skating, weight lifting and lacrosse. When I asked her how mindset impacts performance in sports, she explained to me that:

To an extent, you can allow your mind to get in the way, but we also have the ability to override negative thoughts. Our thoughts aren't all facts. They are giving you a signal of what's going on or how you're feeling, but you have the choice whether you listen to it or not. Mindfulness is learning to observe your thoughts and then you can decide – what am I going to do with this? Is this thought helping me in this situation? We can also have false thoughts and false feelings, so it's important to question them.

All of this brings me back to my original question: Which factors determine our outlook and our perception of the world? And is it possible to retrain our minds?

*

After discovering Dweck's book, I began to lean into the idea that your mindset provides the foundation for everything in your life – from how you view and react to situations, to your ability to learn and improve. I encourage you to dedicate time to considering your own mindset in this context. How often do you think about how your mentality and inner dialogue are impacting your actions, for better or for worse? Are you operating from a default fixed mindset? If so, it's time to make some changes. Remember the brain is malleable, so change is always possible as long as you have the will and desire. But in order to grow, you first have to be open to learning. It's not about pursuing perfection or impossibly high standards. No one is perfect: we all have a unique set of strengths and weaknesses, so forget about perfection and instead focus on *progress*.

A crucial part of the learning process is feedback. Seek honest and accurate feedback from people you trust – this could be a friend, work colleague or mentor – and remind yourself that feedback is essential to help you move closer to your goals. Try not to view negative feedback as criticism, as this will only limit your growth. Draw your attention to your weaknesses in order to figure out what you need to do or who you need to speak to in order to learn and improve, and don't be afraid to ask for help or to admit that you don't have all the answers (yet). Asking questions does not highlight a lack of knowledge; it highlights your willingness to learn. A common trait among high achievers is their commitment to learning. As Stephen Covey, author of the international bestseller *The 7 Habits of Highly Effective People*, says, 'The key to success is dedication to life-long learning.' Whether that's reading books, attending masterclasses or seeking mentorship, the top 10 per cent remain at the top of their game by continuing to learn and develop their skills.

When it comes to learning, there are a number of things to consider. Firstly, let's talk about skill acquisition. Ask yourself: what does it *really* take to master a new skill? Could you learn a new language in a year? How about six months? How about six weeks? Maybe you could, but are you willing to put in the hours?

In his book *Outliers*, the journalist and author Malcolm Gladwell proposes his 10,000-Hour Rule, namely that it takes 10,000 hours to become world-class at anything. So, according to Gladwell, if you dedicate two hours a day to playing a musical instrument, adding up to 728 hours a year, it would take you roughly 13.7 years to become an extraordinary musician. But if you spend eight hours each day playing that instrument, it would take you *just* 3.4 years to achieve that same standard. (I guess I'd better get to work, then.) Although I understand that the idea of doing eight hours a day of dedicated practice might not be the best way to inspire anyone to pick up a violin, what I want you to take away from this is that if you dedicate enough time to something – anything – then you can and will become extraordinary at it, regardless of your shoe size or any other genetic factors you think might hold you back. We all have the potential to become truly extraordinary at pretty much anything, given the right environment and enough time spent on deliberate practice. Reminding yourself of this will reinforce the ideas and the foundations for establishing a growth mindset.

Over the last few decades, access to learning has changed dramatically. Technology and innovation have made it easier than ever to seek out new information. It's not an exaggeration to say that podcasts, audio-books and YouTube videos have changed my life. I am an auditory learner, which means I learn best through listening. I can recall information that I have heard very easily and can often quote things word for word. I remember the way it sounds, due to the rhythm and the intonation of a person's voice. For that reason, listening to a podcast is a much more efficient way for me to learn than reading a book, writing notes or even watching a demonstration. Realising this has allowed me to learn far more quickly, and enjoy the process a lot more too. Plus, I no longer berate myself for my inability to read a whole book in a single weekend, the way my sister can.

There are seven different learning styles, and while some people may have a clear dominant or preferred style of learning, others will use a mix of the following:

Auditory:
You learn best through sound, voice and music.

Visual:
You learn best using imagery, pictures and spatial understanding.

Verbal:
You learn best through speaking, reading or writing.

Physical:
You learn best through movement, mirroring and touch.

Logical:
You learn best by problem-solving, systems and reasoning.

Social:
You learn best with others, or as part of a team.

Solitary:
You prefer to learn and work alone.

It's important to identify which learning style, or combination of styles, is most effective for you, and to consider how this may have impacted your ability to learn earlier in life. I'm sure I would have got better grades at school had I been able to learn via audio content, in solitude. Ironically, for someone who loves to socialise as much as I do, being around others – working in a group or classroom environment, for instance – hinders my ability to focus and learn. I'm easily distracted and I talk too much. (Trust me, every single one of my teachers would agree.) Identifying which learning style suits you could also change the game when it comes to developing your mindset, and specifically your beliefs about your own ability and IQ. Perhaps not achieving high grades at school meant you subconsciously placed limitations on yourself later on in life. You didn't pursue a degree or apply for specific jobs, because deep down you didn't believe that you were smart enough. Finding a new method of learning could unlock skills and talents you didn't even know you had.

*

One of the most empowering things I have ever learned is that I am responsible for my own life. The choices that I make each day have an enormous effect on my health, my relationships, my career, my mistakes, wins, failures – all of it. I'm not discounting the other factors that may contribute to my ability to make certain choices, but ultimately I am in charge of my decisions. Every single person reading this book will have their own unique circumstances and experiences, and there's not a one-size-fits-all approach when it comes to addressing the nuances of individual agency. There are endless structures that influence us to varying degrees – social class, gender, ethnicity, cultural influence, the list goes on – and all of these factors will arguably determine our ability to make decisions, take action and create positive change. It's incredibly difficult to measure how much each of these enhances or inhibits us, and this is a debate that I often have with myself and others. I can only speak from my own perspective – as unique as that may be – and offer ideas and frameworks that I have found useful when exploring this notion of 'individual ownership'. I hope that they will enable you to challenge your thinking and feel empowered to take action in your own life.

When I reflect on my journey so far, I could list a number of things that might be viewed by some as a disadvantage. I am a woman and therefore directly impacted by gender inequality. I am a woman of colour living in the UK and so statistically I can expect to earn 15 per cent less than my white peers. I do not have a degree. I was raised by a single mother with a low income. However, I refuse to allow any of these things to hold me back. I've never even considered the notion that I would be less able to achieve my goals than any-body else. My unique circumstances are not the reason I can or cannot succeed, they are simply the parameters in which I *must*. I try not to compare my situation to that of someone else – it's not a useful exercise and it doesn't get me any closer to my goals. The way I see it, you can either focus on your past circumstances, or you can focus on creating better for your future. You have to make a choice, because you can't do both.

Now I want you to ask yourself: What is *your* mindset when it comes to individual ownership? What's your go-to response when things don't go to plan? Do you look for someone to blame or do you honestly and openly reflect on your own actions, and the role that you played in the outcome? If you don't get that promotion you really wanted, do you blame your boss and look for reasons and excuses ('She's threatened by me', 'He doesn't like me', and so on) instead of taking ownership and asking for feedback that could help you in the future? If your parents didn't give you support and encouragement while you were growing up, if they didn't nurture your passions, do you waste time and energy feeling angry and blaming them for your unhappiness today? Or do you focus on looking forward and ask, 'What are the steps that I can take *now*?' I can boldly say that I have achieved many things in my life – not as a result of my circumstances but *in spite* of them – and I'm not going to allow my past to dictate my future. And neither should you. It's not always easy to think this way, but I believe that the alternative is far less favourable. It can be difficult to take complete ownership of everything in your life, but the reality is that acknowledging and even celebrating this responsibility is a necessary step in adjusting and developing an empowering mindset.

I've discussed these ideas with many of the guests on the Power Hour podcast, including Maggie Alphonsi, a former English rugby union player and *Sunday Times* Sportswoman of the Year. Maggie was born with club foot, a physical disability which means she spent a lot of her childhood in and out of hospital, yet she went on to join the England national team and win the World Cup. For Maggie, it was through playing sports that she developed her mindset, particularly when it came to success and failure, and a philosophy she calls 'live in stretch'.

It's good to know what it feels like to fail. We are very risk-averse and we try our very best to avoid failure. I've learned to embrace failure now. If I make a mistake, I know it's okay because I will grow and learn from it. Taking part in sport and competition creates both success and failure, so you learn how to handle it . . . I always try to live in stretch; it's all about getting comfortable with being uncomfortable. When I got my first opportunity to work for ITV as a pundit on the men's Rugby World Cup back in 2015, I initially thought, *I'm a bit shy, I've never spoken on TV before, and also it's men's rugby so this is outside of my comfort zone.* But then I thought, *You know what? I can do this. I've been playing the sport for a long time, I've won a World Cup! I'm not commentating on a gender, I'm commentating on a sport that I'm a real expert at.* So I said yes and took that step. The first game I was nervous, the second game I was nervous, but eventually it started to click and felt comfortable. So I'm always trying to stretch myself just a little bit further. And not just as a

one-off, but every day or every week I try to find
a new way to be temporarily uncomfortable so
that I can continue to live in stretch.

Words have power and they can have a lasting effect
too. I remember a teacher telling me 'Don't get your
hopes up' when I said I was travelling to London to
audition for a three-year scholarship at a performing
arts school. But rather than allow my teacher's
comment to lower my expectations of what I was
capable of achieving, I think it actually fuelled me
more. That 'I'll prove you wrong' attitude can actually
be really powerful, if channelled correctly. When
I arrived in London for the audition, I was nervous
(who wouldn't be?) but I did not have a single doubt
in my mind that I would be offered a scholarship.
Maybe I was naive, and a little arrogant too. I was
16, after all. But even back then, I was pretty self-
aware – and while I knew that I wouldn't be the most
talented person in the room, I also knew I would
be memorable. While most teenagers just want to be
like everyone else and blend into the crowd, that was
never an option for me as the only black girl in my

class. I was the only girl among my friends with afro hair, and the only girl who knew every single lyric to the Destiny's Child album *The Writing's on the Wall*. ('Say My Name' is iconic.)

I never wanted to stand out at school, but I knew that in an audition it could be a good thing. I could have told myself that my situation growing up (which was, trust me, less than ideal) would hold me back. I hadn't had the years of expensive ballet training that most of the other girls in the room had; I had never had a singing lesson, unless you count belting along to Whitney's greatest hits; and I'd never stepped foot inside a West End theatre before. But rather than imposing limits on myself, my go-to mindset was one of optimism. I really believed that I could, and would, be accepted. Almost 20 years on, a TEDx talk, a hugely successful podcast and a published book later, I still remember that teacher telling me 'Don't get your hopes up'. Words have power and, if I'd been someone else, her statement could have been the beginning and end for me. Instead, six months later I moved to London on my own, aged 16, with a scholarship to attend the Doreen Bird College of Performing Arts – and I never looked back. A year after graduating, I toured the UK in a national musical, and later performed for two years in London's iconic West End show *We Will Rock You*. One thing's for sure: I'll never say 'Don't get your hopes up' to anyone.

I believe creating a positive mantra (like Maggie's 'live in stretch') can be a very powerful tool. One of mine, which I have shared many times and always go back to, is 'You can do hard things'. This is about accepting that it doesn't matter if you're feeling motivated, it doesn't matter how well you're prepared or how many times you've rehearsed, some things are *just bloody hard* and probably always will be. I find that acknowledging and celebrating that is extremely empowering. You're not trying to take a shortcut or find a hack to make life easier, because you know that *you can do hard things*. I've applied this mantra to so many different aspects of my life, from the small to the big things, and it never lets me down. Getting up early every day is hard. Running a marathon is hard. Leading is hard. Being a parent is hard. Quitting an unhealthy habit is hard. Saying no can be hard. I know there's no magic pill that will suddenly make any of those things easy for me, so instead of pretending they'll one day get easier, I acknowledge that, yes, some things are going to be hard – but I can do them anyway. Please feel free to adopt this mantra and use it, share it, declare it and mean it! When your alarm goes off tomorrow morning, *You can do hard things.* When you have to stand up and present a talk, *You can do hard things.* When you need to have a difficult conversation, or ask for help, or admit that you've made a mistake, *You can do hard things.*

*

The mind is incredibly complex, but there are tools, techniques and daily practices that we can learn to help us on our journey to unlocking our full potential. One of the tools used by Jim Kwik, a brain performance expert and author of *Limitless*, is his theory of 'dominant questions.' It's based on the idea that asking yourself certain questions will lead you to certain answers. So, for instance, if you ask yourself, 'Why can I never stick to my workout routine?' or 'How will I ever meet someone and start a relationship, when all I have time for is work?' then your worldview and your interactions with others will be rooted in negativity. These types of questions do not offer solutions, and therefore allow you to remain at a dead end. We all know those people who can't see the good in anything, who are constantly focused on what everyone else has and firmly believe that life is *just harder* for them. They're unlucky, they can't get ahead, the world is against them. Whatever you're suggesting, they've already tried it and it doesn't work. This attitude in turn affects every decision they make and becomes a self-fulfilling prophecy. They start off by saying 'I can't', and this lack of enthusiasm and self-belief often leads to failure, meaning they now more firmly believe they can't, and so on and so forth till the end of time. The good news is that the opposite is also true. If you switch it around and ask yourself the *right* questions, you'll open your mind up to new opportunities and possibilities. For example, if you are asking yourself, 'What's really stopping me from committing to my workout routine?' or 'How can I create more time in my life to meet new people?' then you are searching for solutions rather than looking for reasons to confirm and validate your negative patterns.

I shared an exercise on my podcast which I call 'Six questions to answer before six'. The idea is simple:

when you wake up in the morning, at the very start of your Power Hour, you write down the answers to six simple questions:

1. What energy do I want to have today?

2. Who can I learn from today?

3. Who can I help today?

4. What one thing can I do today to take me closer to where I want to be a year from now?

5. What am I most looking forward to today?

6. What am I most grateful for today?

Whenever I start with this exercise, I always feel calm, focused and optimistic about the day ahead. It's a very simple way to bring my attention to what is important to me and what I need to prioritise that day. In other words, it puts me in the right mindset: it allows me to consider how I will interact with others, how I want to react to different situations, and how I can show up as the best version of myself. In a fast-paced world full of distractions, it's really important to take some time each day to focus on you. It won't take you long to answer these questions, but I would encourage you to write down the answers – don't just run through them in your head. Writing forces you to be considered and focused, and it can be really useful to look back weeks or months later and read what you've written.

Why is it important to answer the questions first thing in the morning? Kwik has many theories about our brain's ability to learn and retain information, which he teaches in workshops and seminars around the world. He explains that if you read a whole page of text and then answer a list of questions about what you have read, you won't recall as much information as if you were shown the questions first, and then given the text to read. By seeing the questions ahead of the text, it puts you at an advantage because you already know which answers you're looking for as you read. I think this applies to my six morning questions too. I bring my attention to the questions first thing, so throughout the day my mind is constantly looking out for the answers I wrote down. In other words, my brain's bias is looking for ways to reinforce my positive mindset. Is it just as good to answer the six questions in the evening before going to bed as a way to reflect back on the day? While I'm sure there is some value in doing that, if you wait until evening then you're looking back instead of looking forward. Whether it was good or bad, you can't change what has already happened. Far better to prime your mind at the start of each day and start as you mean to go on. We've all heard 'ask and you shall receive', so don't be afraid to ask questions: ask for what you want, ask for more, ask for help, *just ask*.

When it comes to creating your own list of dominant questions, write down a variety of different options and see which ones stand out to you. These are the questions that will bring you the most value. My favourite question to answer, for instance, is: 'What am I most looking forward to today?' The answer to that might be watching my son at his after-school athletics practice, or interviewing a new guest on the podcast, or sometimes it will be as simple as having a warm croissant with jam for breakfast after my morning run. What I love about this question is that it encourages me to look for joy in the everyday, and to appreciate that no matter how busy or challenging life gets, there is always something to look forward to.

Here are a few more examples to consider:

> ▸ How can I make today memorable?
>
> ▸ What can I do to reduce my stress or worry today?
>
> ▸ Who would really love to hear from me today?
>
> ▸ What could I do today to improve my health?
>
> ▸ What task have I been putting off that I could complete today?
>
> ▸ How can I have more fun today?
>
> ▸ Who should I say 'thank you' to today?

Remember to ensure your questions are enforcing a growth mindset. Replace 'Why can't I . . .' with 'How can I . . .'

*

Whether we like it or not, everything in our lives is constantly changing. In fact, the only thing that is certain *is* change. Since I first started public speaking and hosting my podcast, one of the most common things people tell me is that they believe it's too late for them to make a change. Surely once you're ten years into a career, it's too late to pivot? Once you're married with kids, isn't it too late to admit you're unhappy? How could you become a runner and get fit if you've spent your adult life avoiding exercise like the plague? I've heard such things again and again, in many different forms and disguises, and met so many people who are held back by the idea that it's simply too late. However, I remain pretty obsessed with the idea that we can always continue to adapt and grow. I've witnessed some extraordinary mindset transformations as a coach, and I've watched people learn how to improve their habits, behaviours and core beliefs. I truly believe that, regardless of where you are today, there is always potential for change.

Before the 1920s, scientists believed that our brain pathways were permanent, and that soon after adolescence the brain would no longer be able to develop new patterns. As a result, cognitive function would decrease as we continued to age. Sounds pretty bleak, right? The good news is that, throughout the twentieth century, psychologists and neuroscientists conducted experiments that definitively concluded that this was simply not true. Our brain is a complex organ that responds very quickly to changes of stimulus, environment, lifestyle and diet. The term 'neuroplasticity' is used to describe the brain's ability to adapt and change – to continue to create new connections and pathways as a result of new experiences. 'Plasticity exists from the cradle to the grave; and . . . radical improvements in cognitive functioning – how we learn, think, perceive, and remember – are possible even in the elderly,' explains Norman Doidge in describing the work of Dr Michael Merzenich, one of the pioneers of neuroplasticity. In other words, I now have scientific proof for one of my core beliefs: *It is never too late.*

It's okay to change your mind too. Changing your mind is not a failure. You can have an idea or a plan that you initially believe is 100 per cent right, only to later learn that it's not that great. Cementing in an idea or a mindset simply because you made one decision a long time ago is a fixed mindset at play. What was right for you then might not be right for you now, and it's okay to rethink or adjust your plan. Society often encourages us to pick and stick, especially when it comes to careers. Traditionally, we have been told that we should focus on one niche area and work towards mastery of it because that's how we achieve 'expert' status. This step-by-step approach of education and learning followed by practice and application was for a long time the perceived formula for success. Climb the ladder, stay in your lane, centre on one thing and know it inside out. And while this might suit you just fine, it's not the only way to become successful, and it's worth reflecting on whether it really is the best route for you – it certainly has never been that way for me. The modern world continues to change at a rapid pace. Technology, digital innovation, social media and modern industry mean that this pick-and-stick approach has quickly become outdated.

When it comes to your career, changing your mind could be perceived by those with a fixed mindset as an indication of flightiness or indecision. The term 'jack of all trades' springs to mind. You might even have heard that having too many different jobs listed on your CV could make you a less attractive candidate and appear disloyal to a potential employer. Personally, I believe that this is the product of an old-school mentality, one that is changing. Someone with a growth mindset would think: *Here is a person who has acquired a diverse skill set – someone who has gained a variety of experience from multiple different perspectives.* 'In a world that is becoming increasingly automated by technology and artificial intelligence, it is our creativity, emotional intelligence and other soft skills that make us, as humans, powerful and relevant,' agrees business coach and founder of Welltodo Global, Lauren Armes. 'We learn these skills through rich and varied life experiences, being courageous and trying new things – all of which a varied career path gives us!' The new world of work will require and applaud these things. Plus, rigid titles and job descriptions will become increasingly redundant in the workplace of the future – where we focus on actual skills and are rewarded for being more flexible in the results that we can deliver. Start-ups especially require this type of person – the kind who can tackle multiple projects from a variety of angles.

You might have been forced to choose a career before being given the chance to figure out what you really enjoy, and what your strengths, weaknesses, creative skills and core values are, all of which essentially dictate the level of fulfilment you will get from certain job roles or working environments. Whether you're thinking about making a career or lifestyle change, or changing your relationships – however big or small that change may be – it takes a lot of courage. Take a deep breath and remember, *you can do hard things*.

If I look back now at the person I was ten years ago, it's very clear that I have changed in so many ways. I've learned a lot in that time, and I hope that I will continue to do so. When someone tells me that I've changed, my response is always 'Thank you'. As someone with a growth mindset, I'm aware that even my fundamental core values and beliefs are not fixed, even if I might sometimes wish they were. Never take 'You've changed' as an insult, because it is impossible to stay the same and it is unhelpful to remain static. Developing a growth mindset is a way to evolve, so don't underestimate your potential for future change. There is nothing wrong with zigging and zagging while searching for a new and better fit. In fact, this process is something I believe many successful people have in common. It's rare that someone's path to success has had a linear trajectory. Most will have got through a long list of things before appearing to have 'made it'. Each detour, bend and curve will give you something valuable to take to the next stage. Experiences, whether good or bad, are never a waste of time. Even failure has a function.

Many pro athletes or famous musicians had a period of 'sampling time' early in their career, though we are quick to discount that they transferred a certain amount of their previous skill from one thing to the next. Roger Federer, for instance, had a very varied experience before committing to tennis. But this is far less widely known than the famous story of Tiger Woods who was holding a golf club before the age of two (there are many videos online of him hitting golf balls with incredible accuracy when he was only four). Woods's father stated that his son would one day be the greatest golfer in the world – and lo and behold, by the age of 21, Tiger Woods had already reached number one in the world rankings by dedicating himself to the sport. This aligns with Gladwell's 10,000-Hour Rule and showcases the benefit of going all-in on a single goal. In contrast, when Federer was growing up in Switzerland he was a huge football fan. He credits much of his tennis career success to the wide range of sports he practised as a child, including swimming, badminton and basketball. He was eight years old when he first picked up a tennis racket. Still incredibly young, of course, but the main difference here is that he continued to play a number of sports throughout his formative years, instead of having a laser-focus approach. He was not made to choose a single activity, but rather encouraged to try lots of different sports.

Even if you were not a child prodigy, you were probably still asked what you wanted to be when you grew up. But how can we expect an eight-year-old to make a decision that could determine their career path for the rest of their lives? For many people, finding their true passion takes time, and they need permission to try different things and make decisions with the freedom of knowing they can change their mind later down the line.

The question you might be asking is: 'How will my decision to make a change affect other people in my life?' How would, say, a vegan diet and lifestyle impact the people that you live with? Will you miss out on socialising with friends or become *that guy* who has to bring his own dessert? What will you say if people question why you're making this change? I'll be honest, feeling concerned about how others will react to my decision to change is something I have struggled with a lot in the past. It's far too easy for people to say, 'Don't worry about what anyone else thinks, forget about them.' I sometimes wish I could take this advice, but the truth is I care deeply about how my actions will affect others, and I care (perhaps a bit too much) about what others think. As I write this book, I am afraid to commit my words to the page, in fear that someone will misinterpret what I'm saying or criticise me for it, so I've had to really work on trusting myself to find the courage to share my ideas with the world. I have to constantly remind myself, *Adrienne – do not worry about the concern of others, you have a very clear intention for writing this book and you are committed to that intention.* So, whether you want to sign up to climb Mount Kilimanjaro or you want to go back to school to learn computer coding, remember why you're making this change and let that give you the confidence to pursue your passion.

*

Brandon Stanton was a financial trader who lost his job in 2010 as a result of the financial crisis. 'My two biggest lessons learned as a trader are take risks and get comfortable with taking losses and setbacks to help move you forward,' he said in an interview with CNBC. This mindset is what ultimately allowed him to embark on a whole new career path. While unemployed and sleeping on a blow-up mattress, Brandon started sharing portrait photography. He had very little photography experience; it was a passion project, which he titled 'Humans of New York'. His photography became insanely popular, and the Humans of New York Instagram page now shares Brandon's photography and the real-life stories he's collected to an audience of over ten million followers. He has published books and now travels the world as a photographer.

For anyone who's just lost their job, it is very difficult to know what to do next, and stories like Brandon's might not seem particularly useful. There are practical issues that come with no longer having an income, which is a real, concrete problem that can't be solved simply by ignoring it and looking on the bright side. Losing your job has many other implications too – it can impact your self-esteem and really knock your confidence. We all have a part of our identity attached to the work we do, so I doubt you're going to be delighted and immediately start celebrating, but it's also true that it can be a catalyst for necessary change that you might not otherwise have made. Once you assess all of your options, you have no choice but to take action: you must either sink or swim. Having a growth mindset will lead you to look for ways to make this a change for the better, turning a perceived failure into an opportunity.

The ultimate endurance athlete James Lawrence (known as 'the Iron Cowboy') believes everyone should experience hitting rock bottom at some point in their life. According to James, only then will you be forced to really assess your life and make the changes you need. I'm not sure if I completely agree with James – I wouldn't wish extreme adversity on anyone – but I can understand his point. The reality is that, when you reach rock bottom, you have nothing to lose, meaning you're no longer afraid of what might happen. For most of us, it is fear that stops us from changing. In the past I've asked myself what I would do if I were no longer afraid to fail, or of other people's opinions, judgement or criticism. What if the thing you fear the most has already happened? Don't let that paralyse you. Get real about your relationship with fear if you want to understand your own mindset. Fear is often what keeps us stuck, and it could prevent you from ever reaching your full potential.

One person who is no stranger to fear and change is an amazing man who I now call a friend, Karl Lokko. Karl refers to himself as an 'ex-caterpillar', referencing the opening of his TEDx talk (which has now been viewed by almost 100,000 people) in which he recites a poem about his story of transformation from a caterpillar to a butterfly. A former gang leader who grew up on London's Myatts Field estate, Karl witnessed his first shooting at the age of 12. He went on to be shot at, stabbed, cut across the face, and watched his friends being murdered. Karl told me that he once saw his schoolfriend's father stabbed to death over a £50 PlayStation game. As a young man, it seemed there were only two doors open to him: jail or death. It wasn't until the intervention of a Christian leader and a church-run anti-youth-violence project that Karl was able to denounce his gang involvement and transform his life entirely. Today, Karl is an activist, poet and highly successful public speaker. A few years ago, he became an advisor to Prince Harry, the Duke of Sussex. He works to reform gang culture and fight for social justice, and his work alongside Richard Branson has raised hundreds of thousands for charity.

In order to make such a dramatic transformation, Karl had to make personal sacrifices and abstain from his old life, old behaviours and even his former friends.

This is certainly not an easy thing for anyone to do. He created intentional daily rituals – such as reading, prayer and fasting – to break out of the cycle he was in. For him, fasting was a deliberate act, to practise discipline.

I made a decision, I actually made a decision to change. It's not just about the food. Because if you just go without food and water you're just starving, so for me, instead of starving, in order for it to be fasting I had to also be mindful. It was a conscious choice and an awareness of God.

He also became a voracious learner to improve his vocabulary and his ability to express himself, and set out to find mentorship from business leaders and people with social influence by having one-to-one lunch meetings with someone new every week. In other words, he started exercising both his body and his mind. Like many others, he developed an early-morning routine as part of that process:

I got up at 4:00am every day for a year and it was my power. I would wake up each morning and I would pray. There was a stillness that you can't find at 5:00am – trust me, I looked, but I couldn't find it at 5:00am or 6:00am. For me, at 4:00am the world was still and minimal, cars weren't moving around, neighbours' televisions weren't on, and it's quite cold at that time. Everything just added up to making it a very peaceful and spiritual time for me. Then at 5:00am, I would spend a whole hour reading, which left me feeling inspired and wanting more inspiration, so I would then watch a TED talk online. Finally, I would write out a plan for the day.

He began a relentless pursuit of excellence, and each positive change led to another, and another, and another. Karl's willingness to learn and to ask questions ultimately set him on a new trajectory, one in which he had a limitless mindset.

When I interviewed Karl for the podcast, he described the process of change as painful, comparing it to the pain of childbirth. We resist change so much because it's hard and uncomfortable, but, as Karl's experience exemplifies, the reward on the other side of that temporary pain is immeasurable. Karl's story is incredible, and hearing him speak about it gives me chills. He has a way with words and he speaks with so much conviction and raw truth. Karl is living proof that it is never too late. Where you start is not where you will finish. Begin by shifting and changing your mindset, and who knows the impact it could have on your life. The truth is, there's only one way to find out. There are a limitless number of possibilities and potential outcomes, but you have to make the decision to take action and make a change.

When it comes to developing a growth mindset, begin with an honest assessment of where you are currently, and ask yourself if you believe change is possible. Before you answer, consider that whatever you decide – yes or no – *will make it true.* For what it's worth, I'd rather try and fail than look back and think, *What if?* I'm only going to experience my life once, so I have to go after those big goals. I owe it to myself to chase those passions – and I can't wait until my son has grown up, or I have more money, or I get a vague feeling that 'the time is right'. The perfect time doesn't exist, so I'm not even going to wait until tomorrow – because too often, tomorrow stays tomorrow. Shift your mindset away from negativity and fixed limitations; shift it towards growth, possibility and abundance. Create a life that you love and start living it today.

The words we say to ourselves are important; the words we say *about* ourselves even more so.

How to Create Powerful Habits

Forming habits is human nature. We all have habits that we typically label as either 'good' or 'bad', but I like to think of habits as either 'useful' or 'non-useful'. A *useful* habit is an action or behaviour that, when repeated over time, will give you the long-term outcome that you want. On the other hand, a *non-useful* habit, instead of helping you achieve your long-term goals, offers an immediate outcome or short-term reward.

For example, say you've decided you want to get up early and do a yoga class before going to work. You have a clear reason to get up earlier than usual: you know that exercising in the morning means you arrive at the office in a better mood and with more energy. Fast-forward to 5:30am. Your alarm goes off, and you reach out with one arm to turn it off. Your bedroom is dark, and it's cold, so instead of getting out of bed, you bury down deep under your warm comfy duvet. You vow you'll do a yoga class in the evening instead. Or maybe you can do the class tomorrow. *It's no big deal, it's just one day, so it doesn't really matter*, you tell yourself. Plus, you're tired, and surely an extra hour in bed is exactly what you need. Yes, in the moment it might be nice to stay in bed, and maybe you even feel happy with this decision. But 12 hours later, you've had a busy day at work, you've still got at least ten things on your to-do list, you feel more frazzled than ever and you're just not in the mood for yoga. This cycle continues in much the same way every day, until a month has passed and you are yet to step foot onto a yoga mat. Sound familiar?

It's very easy to see why we often fall into the pattern of choosing the non-useful habit. We prioritise how we want to feel *now*, over how we want to feel *in the future*. A question that I'm often asked is: 'What about listening to your body and having self-compassion?' My response echoes that same sentiment: are you being compassionate to yourself right now, and giving in to your immediate desires, or are you choosing the more difficult option but being compassionate to your future self? This same tendency typically applies to many of our choices – from picking the sugary quick fix instead of prepping a healthy snack, to replying 'maybe' to an RSVP when we really should have said 'no'. (How many times have you replied 'maybe' to an invitation due to a feeling of obligation, only to regret it when the day of the event comes? *Note to self – stop doing that.*) Most of our non-useful habits are routine solutions to problems we've encountered many times before – so, for instance, if I'm hungry, I'll eat a snack; if I'm bored, I'll look at my phone; if I'm stressed, I'll pour a glass of wine. You get the gist. Common phrases such as 'annoying habits' or 'bad habits' suggest that doing things repeatedly is a negative thing – but there is an equal amount of benefit to be gained from habits too. Whenever I'm driving or commuting on the train, I listen to audiobooks. This has become something that I do automatically – as soon as I sit down, I reach for my headphones. I've made learning a habit. It's important to remember that, regardless of whether you have repeated the same non-useful habit for weeks, months or even years, it is always possible to replace it with a new, better and more useful one.

Then there are what I like to call 'powerful habits'. In short, powerful habits have a much greater impact than 'normal' habits. They have a knock-on effect on other aspects of your life: the action itself might be small, but it could be the first in a long series of dominos to fall. A powerful habit will affect your next decision, and the next, and the next. Many of our habits will create an onward spiral effect, for better or for worse, but a powerful habit is one that has an immeasurable impact. Personally speaking, creating powerful habits is what has given me a disproportionate advantage. I didn't get a head start in life, and I've never had a fast-track pass to the finish line. The elevator has never been an option for me – I've always had to take the stairs. In every area of my life, from training to be a professional dancer to building a podcast audience, progress has always been incremental and slow. If I'm being honest, I don't have any extraordinary talents or skills, but if there is one thing I can say with certainty, it is that I am consistent. I practise the same things again and again. I create powerful habits – and trust me, over time, the small things matter.

*

In the last 60 years, scientists and psychologists have made significant advances in understanding behavioural change and habit formation. In *The Power of Habit*, Charles Duhigg popularised the theory of the 'habit loop': a three-step loop which explains what is happening within our brains when habits are formed. First, there is a cue, triggering a response. Then our response becomes a routine behaviour, and this can be physical, mental or emotional. Finally, there is the reward, which is immediate. Our brain remembers that loop, and we are conditioned to repeat it next time we receive that same cue again. Duhigg uses the response to a plate of cookies as an example:

Cue:
Someone walks into the office with a plate of cookies and offers you one.

Response:
'Sure, why not?' Cookies taste great and they are a welcome distraction from looking at your computer screen.

Reward:
You get a sugar high and a temporary dopamine rush as you eat the cookie and chat with friends.

The theory is that your brain will remember this positive reward, and therefore when presented with the same cue in the future – a plate of cookies – your response will be the same too: eat the cookies.

More recently, James Clear, the author of *Atomic Habits*, suggested that there is one more step in the middle. Clear identified that sometimes the same cue does not trigger the exact same response. We may react differently depending on our mood, our emotional state, our environment. Using the cookie example again, let's say you've recently been to the dentist and, after examining your teeth, she advised you to reduce the amount of sugary foods in your diet. As a result, the next time the plate of cookies comes around in the office, you might be tempted at first, but then you remember the dentist's advice and decline the offer. The cue was the same, but this time your response was different. A week later, when offered the plate of cookies again, you might say yes – it's only one cookie after all. In other words, the response isn't consistent.

As things change and vary, so too will our behaviour, which is what makes changing our behaviour so difficult. We are not computers; we can't just erase one pattern and copy and paste in a new one. (At least, not yet.) There is incredible complexity and nuance to our experience each day: fatigue, stress and emotions often impact our immediate decision-making. However, just because it's hard doesn't mean it's impossible, and it certainly doesn't mean it's not worth doing. This is why I believe having a focused goal is so important. Once we're clear on what our goal is, then we can figure out which of our habits is going to help us to get there. I'm sorry to say that, typically, this *isn't* the habit that will give you the immediate reward, but the one that will benefit you in the long term. For example, going to bed before 10:00pm every night is a good habit if you want to get up early every day. It's not always what you want to do, especially if at 9:55pm you're halfway through watching an episode of *Game of Thrones*. When you switch off the TV in favour of sleep, you don't get an immediate reward, but you'll be glad you've done so when your alarm goes off the next morning.

In other words, doing the hard thing is going to serve you better in the long run, so avoid the urge to take the easy option. In today's world of on-demand services, instant access and warp-speed communication, there are countless temptations to take the shortcut. Our buy-now-pay-later culture has been made even easier by one-click purchasing, and it can quickly fool you into bad spending habits. We want the instant reward of a new phone or a pair of shoes, even if we can't afford to pay for them. Buying things on credit and encouraging debt is a habit that can lead to serious consequences, and is another example of how the small things add up. This is where practising delayed gratification can really make a difference. As Dr Maxwell Maltz explains: 'The ability to discipline yourself to delay gratification in the short term, in order to enjoy greater rewards in the long term, is the indispensable prerequisite for success.'

When it comes to habit formation, the first question people typically ask is 'How long does it take to form a new habit?' Most people want to know how long they will need to put thought, effort and willpower into their new commitment before it becomes automatic and habitual. Well, sadly, the jury is still out. Some people suggest creating a new habit takes as little as five days, while others claim that it takes 30 days. Some even say the magic number is a good 90 days. The conclusion I've drawn from reading all of these different opinions is that it takes as long as it takes. Habits and behaviours are complex and individual – it's not one-size-fits-all. Some people really enjoy routine and structure, while others prefer a more intuitive and responsive approach. Some people can eat half a chocolate brownie and then 'save the rest for later'. (This behaviour is shocking to me. These people are a strange and rare breed.)

I am the sort of person who will have either the whole brownie or no brownie. With everything that I do in my life, I'm either giving it 100 per cent or I'm not doing it at all. In some ways, this is a blessing, as it allows me to set strict rules and means that I work well to deadlines. I can be almost robotic when it comes to setting habits that I don't really enjoy, because I know that they will deliver the long-term outcome I want. A small example is that I made a decision years ago to never stand when I'm on an escalator and to always walk to the top. When you consider that I work in London most weekdays, taking the Underground to meetings and events on opposite sides of the city, I get a lot of opportunities to practise this habit. I've made it something that's non-negotiable: it doesn't matter if it's the end of the day and I'm feeling tired, if I'm carrying a heavy bag (or three) or if I'm wearing heels. I'm walking. You might be thinking, *What's the big deal? It's just an escalator!* Say I walk an average of 60 steps on an escalator, four times a day, five days a week. In a year that amounts to 62,400 steps, or the equivalent of 28 miles! That's further than a marathon. Yes, it's a small daily habit, but those small steps all add up. Don't disregard them, because your daily habits could be having a much greater impact on your life than you realise.

*

Each day, we are faced with thousands of decisions. The world offers us an abundance of choices. Even when dealing with a supposedly simple task like ordering a coffee, there are about 16 different questions you're expected to answer. What size would you like? Which milk? Decaf? Eat in or take away? Do you have your own cup? Would you like a croissant to go with it? Extra shot? Extra-hot? Do you have a loyalty card? Cash or card? What is your name? Would you like to donate a percentage of the cost of your coffee to a charity that will recycle this napkin? 'Sorry can you repeat all of that, I was trying to decide whether to say "yes" or "no" to the croissant.'

This constant decision-making happens throughout the day, whether you realise it or not. It would be impossible to consider each choice individually and assess each possible outcome – so that's when our habits kick in. You don't *decide* to clean your teeth in the morning, you just do it. It's automatic.

Unfortunately, not all habits come as easily as brushing our teeth in the morning. A professional sports player will spend hours and hours repeating the same drills and technical exercises, practising specific movements *off* the pitch so that they can be automatic *on* the pitch. There are multiple variables to consider in the middle of a game, so when a tennis player is waiting to receive a serve from their opponent, they can't be thinking about every single detail of their return hit: when to step forwards, how much to rotate their hips, the angle of the racket, where to look, even when to breathe. These are the tiny but essential decisions that have to be made in less than a second. Instead, they will have spent hours practising, so that their instant reaction comes as a result of memories created through repetition. Similarly, if you want a new habit to become automatic, first you have to practise, which will require effort, deliberate actions and an initial amount of willpower.

The concept of 'willpower' has always been fascinating to me. When I consider what some ultramarathon runners are able to endure – running insane distances over some of the toughest terrains in the world – it makes me wonder, what really *is* willpower? Sport scientists and nutritionists can measure an athlete's aerobic capacity and their heart rate reserve, using them to calculate calorie expenditure and estimate the athlete's potential 'limits', but no scientist will ever be able to quantify a person's will. Some call it 'grit' or 'determination', but whatever this elusive willpower is, I want to know: Why do some people have more than others? And how can we all get more of it?

When I asked chartered psychologist Fiona Murden to break down the science behind willpower, she likened it to a muscle. She explained that, in the same way we train a muscle to make it stronger, we can train to increase our willpower too. If you want to increase the size of a muscle, then you need to add resistance – and it's the same when it comes to training willpower. So how do you add resistance? Well, start with something simple like swearing. Challenge yourself not to swear for a whole week – and every time you feel the urge to swear, resist it. If you need a visible incentive, go old-school and establish a swear jar in which you add £1 each time that you swear (this cash must be donated to charity or given to your kids as pocket money at the end of the week). The point of this is less about swearing itself, and more a simple way to exercise your willpower muscle by resisting automatic responses or habits.

Just like any muscle, the more we use willpower, the more tired it gets. This explains why you can say no to something and mean it the first time you're asked, but you are far more likely to give in by the third or fourth time. Many parents know this all too well. (Many three-year-olds know this too.) So if the good news is that we can all get more willpower, the bad news is that, yet again, it's something that will require effort on our part. Fiona suggested that, once you decide to establish a new useful habit, you need to commit to it 100 per cent and make it absolutely non-negotiable (like my avoiding escalators), essentially eliminating any element of choice or decision-making. If you repeat one thing consistently every single day, it's only a matter of time before it becomes automatic, but you have to be willing to show up and do the hard part first.

If motivation and discipline are just a part of habit formation, then what makes up the rest? Many of us also need accountability. I recently discovered that 'accountability coaches' are a real thing. You pay somebody – a lot of money, I might add – to check up on you multiple times throughout the day in order to ensure you are in fact doing what you said you would. (I'm not sure what bothers me the most: knowing there are people spending money on this, or knowing others are accepting it.) You send them photos: post-workout selfies, pictures of your meals and whatnot. In return, the accountability coach sends you messages to prompt and praise you for your efforts. If this sounds appealing, keep in mind that your mum would probably jump at the opportunity to do this for free! I am of course partly joking (mums are a nightmare), but I do find the idea of an accountability coach problematic, especially considering the potentially toxic relationship to exercise and food that this arrangement could trigger. Personally, I think you are doing yourself a disservice if you believe you need someone to check in on you as though you were a child, and it really won't benefit you in the long run. You are in control of your own choices, so avoid the temptation to pass the responsibility on to somebody else. By paying someone to enforce your routine for you, you are essentially outsourcing answerability and skipping a big part of the process. It's crucial that you learn how to create a routine and stick to it. Are you going to pay this person forever, whenever you want to achieve *anything*? If not, how will you continue this new routine, or start another one, without them? You have to be able to trust yourself and your ability to make the best decision. You have to show up and do the work for yourself. This is your life, no one else's.

What about getting an accountability buddy instead – a friend you know will motivate you and help keep you on track? If you are drawn to the idea, then I challenge you to also flip that concept on its head. Why don't *you* become someone's accountability buddy? Instead of asking a friend to join you in your new routine to ensure that *you* show up, why not reach out to someone you know who needs encouragement or maybe even someone to lead them? Showing up for them is a great way to show up for yourself too – and doing something in service of others is always a good thing to do.

*

Powerful habits can take many forms, and some are more impactful than others. A powerful habit that will leave a lasting impression is being conscious of the words you use most frequently. Words have power! What you say out loud is a declaration, and regardless of whether it's actually *true*, that declaration will steer you in one of two directions.

Imagine you're arriving at work in the morning and a member of your team stops you to ask, 'Hey, how are you?' What is your response? Or when you pick your kids up from school, or greet your partner at the end of each day, what is the first thing you say? Do you consider the power of your words and responses? Or do you have a habit of replying with the same answer again and again and again:

'How are you?'

'I'm fine.' 'I'm tired.' 'I'm mega busy.' 'I'm stressed.'

Your choice of words will impact your mood, your actions and your habits. If your automatic response is that you're tired, stressed out or too busy, then it is important to recognise this and ask yourself why. Are you actually tired every day? Are you really stressed out all the time? Are you too busy every single moment? If the answer is 'yes', then ask yourself: What are the consequences? Can you keep living your life like this? What can you do to change it? More likely, it's not really accurate, and it's just something you say without much thought. If that's the case, then consider it to be the first habit you need to replace. Declaring you are tired and stressed out every day will affect your choices and your behaviour. You'll always be 'too tired' to work out and 'too stressed' to take time off, therefore trapping yourself in this narrative.

With this in mind, the next time someone asks you how you are, I want you to pause and think about your answer rather than speaking out of habit. Try to start responding with something positive, and then go one step further and ask *them* a positive question. One of my favourite things to ask people is 'What are you most looking forward to this week?' or 'What are you most excited about right now?' And for any parents, this is also a great way to connect with your kids. When I pick my son up from school, if I ask him how his day was, he'll usually give me a pretty short and vague answer: 'It was good' or 'It was okay'. So, instead, I ask him things like 'Who did you sit next to at lunchtime today?' or 'What was the best thing that happened at school today?' It not only gives me an opportunity to learn about his classmates, to hear his perspective and to find out what he's enjoying at the moment, but also – and most importantly – it encourages him to recall something good about his day. This is a powerful habit that I want him to build: reflecting on the day and focusing on the highlights. Plus, sharing them with someone else is a great way to cement joyful memories and relive positive and meaningful experiences.

The words we say to ourselves are important; the words we say *about* ourselves even more so. Talking negatively about ourselves is a non-useful habit, and I guarantee that saying things like 'I'm never going to be able to do this' is itself the reason you won't be able to do it. Putting yourself down isn't going to take you closer to any of your goals, so why do it? It's often a form of self-defence or self-preservation: if we set the bar low and limit our expectations, then we can save ourselves from the pain of disappointment. But how about if you were to reverse this thinking? Have you ever thought that maybe your goals are actually too small, and you have the potential to go ten times bigger? Every time you notice that negative inner voice, pause and ask yourself: is this true? Here's a challenging thought – maybe it *is* true. If you keep saying you're lazy then maybe it's because you actually are lazy, but that doesn't mean that you can't change. You have to either accept it or change it. You can't do both. If you are repeating the same words to yourself day after day, for better or for worse, make sure those words are true.

I have a confession to make. Years ago, when I first heard someone talking about the power of positive affirmations, I sighed and I rolled my eyes. The idea that simply saying a sentence out loud, regardless of whether or not you believe it to be true, would somehow make it true didn't sit well with me. I was sceptical and found the whole concept of 'positive language' a bit patronising. I challenged the idea that speaking words of positivity would somehow change everything in your life no matter how bad your circumstances were. Growing up, I had to take on a lot of responsibility at a young age. My mother never sugar-coated things, and she never apologised for our situation. Her attitude was always that you just had to get on with it, whether you liked it or not. I needed to help take care of my younger siblings, and so I quickly saw the reality of daily life. I became very independent, and in doing so I learned that meritocracy is essentially a myth. Life *isn't* fair, no matter how much we wish it were. I don't say that with any bitterness – I don't go through life with a chip on my shoulder. But what I want to make clear is that I grew up knowing life wasn't going to be like a Disney movie. The good guy doesn't always show up to fix everything at the end, the underdog doesn't always triumph and, to debunk possibly the biggest lie of all, frogs do not turn into princes. Perhaps that's why I've never enjoyed reading novels. My younger sister adores reading; I remember when she got the fourth Harry Potter book, the really big one. She was only nine years old and she read the entire book in just a few days. Meanwhile, I couldn't understand how she could be so invested in the fictional lives of fictional characters (let alone accept the fact that they were witches and wizards). To be honest, I still don't really enjoy reading fiction. I much prefer biographies and memoirs – maybe I just like to know that what I'm reading about is real.

I think my initial scepticism towards positive affirmations was due to thinking that the point of reciting an affirmation over and over again was to fool you into believing that it was somehow suddenly true. If you stand in front of the mirror each morning and say 'I am confident', does that actually make you more confident? Maybe. But how about if you say 'I am growing taller' – will you grow taller? Or will saying 'I am a millionaire' make your bank balance change? Probably not. The truth is, I could stand outside and say the sky is green again and again, but it won't change the fact that the sky is blue. Looking back now, I realise I was missing the point. Our brain knows the difference between what is true and what isn't; we know what is real and what is pretend. The practice of positive affirmations is not about trying to convince yourself to believe something false, it's about focusing on the good, about shifting your attention away from negative – and potentially destructive – thoughts. It often doesn't matter what you look at, only what you *see*. Practising positive affirmations will redirect your focus and rewire your thinking towards positivity, and in doing so will help you to create a new reality.

The average person speaks around 7,000 words each day. Now, ask yourself: What are you saying to yourself and others? How are your words impacting your mood? Are they encouraging and uplifting? What is the story you want to tell? Are your words truthful? Do you really mean what you say? If I'm going to say 7,000 words today, I want them to be the *right* ones, and for them to have a positive impact. I want my words to become affirmations. I want to speak words that will add value to my mind, my relationships, my experiences and my world.

*

I want to share a few of my most useful and non-useful habits, but note that this is a judgement-free zone!

My most non-useful habit by far, that I sometimes think could border on addiction, is checking my phone. That's right, I'm putting my hand up and admitting it. This is a book about powerful habits, self-mastery, motivation and discipline, but I am only human and I too succumb to the seductive stream of social approval, likes, direct messages, funny memes and WhatsApp messages. In fact, while I was writing this chapter, I had to switch my phone to silent and leave it in another room to avoid distraction.

I was speaking at an event last year and another guest on the panel, Tanya Goodin, revealed that most of us now have our phones within a one-metre radius of our bodies at all times, 24 hours a day. Even more shocking, I think, was when she said that the hormonal response we experience when we lose our phone is initially the exact same response you would have if you lost your child in a busy shop. Don't get me wrong, at least 50 per cent of the time I spend on my phone is useful, and social media has allowed me to build a career and share my voice. I'm certainly not someone who demonises tech and our use of it. However, the other 50 per cent of the time is often wasted, providing an easy distraction that sometimes steals my attention away from more important things, like reading or sleep. There have been times when I've got into bed at 9:30pm with the intention of reading until 10:00pm, only to get into a WhatsApp group chat for ten minutes and then spend another ten minutes watching Instagram stories, before finally putting my phone down, opening my book and realising that it's now 9:52pm. If I continued this cycle every day, I doubt that I'd be able to read a single book in a whole year!

I've now created a cut-off time for my phone use. At 9:30pm, I switch my phone to silent and leave it in the hallway. The first few times I did this, I had a nagging feeling that I should go and check it one more time before bed, just in case. Just in case . . . what? Well, perhaps some sort of emergency, I would tell myself. The reality is that it's very unlikely you will miss something urgent between the hours of 10:00pm and 5:00am. Of course, there are always exceptions: if you're waiting for a pregnant family member to go into labour, or you have an ill grandparent in the hospital. But exceptional circumstances aside, the reality is most things will still be there in the morning and you're really not missing out on anything by staying away from your phone. *Forget the FOMO, Adrienne, read your book and go to bed.*

In terms of my most useful habits, on the other hand, a few obvious ones spring to mind. For instance, before I go to bed, I always plug in my watch and my headphones to recharge. On the floor next to the plug socket, I put my sports bra, leggings, top, running jacket and my face cream. This habit is without a doubt one of the most powerful and useful habits in my routine. When I wake up in the morning, I don't have to waste time stumbling around in the dark looking for my kit, and I don't have to worry about getting halfway through my run and suddenly having my headphones dying on me. (Trust me, it's devastating. You have to persevere with no tunes, no audiobook and no vibe.) Lastly, that little pot of face cream is an essential part of my early-morning run prep. I run during all seasons, and running in the wind, rain and sun can accelerate your skin's ageing process. To be honest, I didn't really care much about this in my twenties, but in the last few years I've become much more aware of the importance of protecting my skin. In an attempt to preserve my complexion for as long as possible, I use an SPF moisturising face cream every morning. It's a small habit but I'm pretty sure that it's working, or at least I hope it is (smug gold star for me). And most importantly, prepping all of these things – which takes no longer than five minutes – means I'm not faced with any decision-making at 5:00am. I know that running will have a positive impact on the rest of my day, I've experienced it time and time again, and having everything laid out ready in front of me means there is zero brainpower required. I created this powerful habit because it means I no longer need to rely on motivation either – I simply get up and go into automatic mode.

When it comes to creating your own powerful habits, I believe there are three steps you need to take.

Step one: *Assess your current daily habits. Assign them as either 'useful' or 'non-useful'.*

The first thing you need to do is figure out what your current habits are, and whether they are useful or non-useful. Think of this as Marie Kondo-ing your habit wardrobe.

Take a blank piece of paper or a notebook and write down what you actually do in an average day. Break it down hour by hour, and make sure to note down everything. Be really honest, and remember no one is ever going to read this paper and judge you. Don't even judge yourself when you're doing this exercise. This is not about perfection or about making every single hour productive, it's simply an audit of your time, which is your most valuable currency.

Look at the list, and ask yourself: Which habits are stealing your time? Which habits take more energy than they give? Which habits make you feel bad about yourself? These are the ones that have got to go.

On the other side of the coin, determine which those habits are that you want to keep up and maybe even do more of. Which habits are making you healthier? Which habits are making you a better parent, partner, grandchild, friend? Which habits are helping you create a life that you love?

Step two: *Adapt, replace or recreate, new, better, more powerful habits.*

If you want to make a new habit, a good place to start is by attaching it to something you're already doing. This is particularly useful because it doesn't require you to 'make more time'. Trying to simply find more time in your schedule is not the best way to cement a new habit. Instead, just make the most of the time you've got.

For instance, if you walk for 15 minutes each day to the train station, what habit could you piggyback onto that walking time? Maybe you could use that time to call your parents or a friend, or listen to a podcast or an audiobook. Or it might be that it's a good time for silence and solitude, to stimulate reflection and mindfulness. And it doesn't even have to be on that big a scale. Think about the time you spend waiting for the kettle to boil. What do you do with those two minutes? Could you do some deep belly breaths to calm your nervous system, or some stretches? Attaching a new habit to your existing routine means you're far more likely to do it.

When it comes to food and diet – an area where many people struggle to make good habits – it can be helpful to *replace* a habit instead of trying to abolish it altogether. If you want to drink less alcohol during the week and you usually drink a glass of wine (or two) after dinner in the evening, try replacing it with sparkling water or a non-alcoholic G&T instead. This way, you can still continue to enjoy the daily ritual, and reduce your alcohol intake at the same time.

It's important to think about *how* you want to implement your new habits. Do you like to break things down and introduce changes gradually, or do you prefer to make a 180-degree pivot overnight? Everyone is different and it doesn't matter which way you decide to do it, but you need to be mindful and pick the one that is going to set you up for success.

Lastly, consider how many new habits you want to introduce at the same time. Making changes to our behaviour can be really hard, and too much too soon can often be overwhelming. No doubt you will resist the changes at first, and later on you might even find ways to self-sabotage, so make sure you pick the habits that are going to make the biggest impact, and focus on those in the first instance.

Step three: *Add friction: make bad habits harder to choose.*

Let's say one of your non-useful habits is scrolling through social media apps. It often takes up a lot of time – commuting on the train, waiting in line for a coffee, lying on the sofa in the evening – and you've decided you want to reduce your daily usage. The way to do that is to add friction to the process, and make it something that requires more effort. You could, for example, change the settings on your phone so that you are required to enter your password every time you open the app. It's a small change, but entering your password will force you to pause for a moment, meaning opening the app is no longer an automatic habit but an intentional decision. Are you going to enter your password 20 times per day? It's very likely that by adding this small step of friction, your screen time will be reduced.

Similarly, adding friction to your food and exercise habits is a great way to make it easier to choose the useful habit. As obvious as it sounds, if you want to improve your diet and eat less junk food, you have to make sure that you don't have junk food in the house. It really is that simple. After dinner, when you're searching the kitchen for something sweet, if the ice cream is there then you're going to have to call on that willpower muscle again. If there is no ice cream in the house and you really want it, you're going to have to walk or drive to a shop to get it. Add friction and put the non-useful habit a little bit further out of reach.

*

We all have habits that we repeat day after day. If we are not intentional about creating them, then we will most often choose the path of least resistance and go for the easy option – that's just human nature. Your habits impact everything from commitment to exercise and diet, to saving money and making the most of your time. Once you have established powerful habits, you no longer need to rely on willpower and motivation. Creating powerful habits is critical if you want to excel and unlock your true potential.

I have
a purpose
and I'm
moving
towards it.

The Power of Movement

One of the elements of my Power Hour that has had the biggest impact on my life is movement. Movement is essential for both our minds and our bodies, and having a regular physical movement practice – anything from running to yoga to dancing – will enhance so many areas of your life. From boosting your self-confidence, to stress management, to reducing your risk of illness and disease, the benefits of movement are endless. Today's leading doctors, nutritionists and psychologists are in agreement that the lack of movement caused by a sedentary lifestyle is contributing to many of our largest problems, and on a global scale. If we all moved more, we would see a significant reduction in the number of people suffering from obesity-related illnesses. Walking, running and cycling, instead of commuting in cars or on trains, would lower our carbon footprint. Our mental health could also improve as a result of regular physical activity, not to mention the associated health benefits of being outside more often and connecting with others in group activities. There are many lifestyle factors that influence our overall health status, but the key takeaway is that whether you're young or old, black or white, fat or thin, there is not a single person who wouldn't benefit from daily movement.

I use the term 'movement' instead of 'exercise' intentionally. 'Exercise' has so many associations – gyms, bootcamp-style workouts, and tanned, toned, semi-naked personal trainers on Instagram. It might fill you with dread as you flashback to PE classes at school, and being forced to run across a muddy field in freezing-cold wind and rain. Or maybe you're just not an 'exercise' person. You don't own a pair of running shoes and occasionally walking up the escalator on the Underground is the extent of your fitness regime. But no matter how you feel about the *word* 'exercise', the truth is you need movement for both your body and your mind. When I spoke to Dr Rupy Aujla, an NHS doctor and the author of *The Doctor's Kitchen*, he was unequivocal about the fact that regular movement has a positive impact on our health, and he suggested daily movement as one of his principles for living well. 'You don't need to follow an intense daily exercise regimen,' he told me. 'Variety, very much like food, is what your body will appreciate.' Another guest on the podcast, chartered psychologist Kimberley Wilson, recently published a book titled *How to Build a Healthy Brain*. In it, she explains how 'movement protects the brain. Physical activity will improve brain blood flow, which is associated with better cognitive performance, focus and attention. Regular exercise has been shown decisively to: reduce the risk of developing depression and anxiety, delay and reverse brain ageing and increase our resilience to stress.' She goes on to state that 'all forms of activity count; the emphasis is simply to move.'

So, for now, let's forget about exercise and instead return to the word 'movement'. Movement is instinctive, it's something our bodies *want* to do. Think about how your body feels when you've been sitting for hours on a long-haul flight, and how good it feels to stand up and stretch your back and move your hips once the seatbelt sign goes off. When you're feeling tired, isn't it amazing to stretch your arms up over your head and let out a really big yawn? Our bodies were made to move. Much of our ability to survive as a species depends on it: our ability to travel, to eat, to communicate and even to procreate – they all require movement. If you have a pet cat or dog, pay attention to what they do right before they go to sleep and when they wake up. Before sleeping, they stretch their entire body from head to toe. (They don't call it 'downward dog' for nothing.) When they wake up, they stretch again, before moving towards daylight and looking for water. Your schedule might be a little busier than your dog's, but she definitely has her priorities right.

Movement has the power to impact so much more than just the shape and size of our bodies – from the way we interact with others, to what we believe is possible for ourselves and our lives.

*

When you start to incorporate movement into your daily Power Hour, it's important to understand that different types of movement will affect your state of mind differently.

I'm sure that you'll have heard of 'runner's high' before, but if you haven't, it's a term used to describe the feeling of euphoria many people experience after going for a run. There is a real physical and chemical shift happening in our brains and bodies when we do roughly 20 minutes of moderate-intensity exercise, with our body releasing the 'happy' hormones dopamine, serotonin and endorphins. (By 'moderate', I mean your heart rate is up and you're breaking a sweat.) This change in state affects the body as well as the brain, in a two-way cognitive feedback loop also known as 'proprioceptive feedback'. Basically, it means our movements impact our state of mind, and vice versa. There are endless ways to include movement in your Power Hour, everything from walking your dog to surfing – remember it's not just about 'working out' – but for now, I'm going to outline the key benefits of just three kinds of movement: low-intensity or low-impact movement, such as yoga; strength training, such as weight lifting; and cardiovascular movement, such as running.

If you choose to begin your day with 30 minutes of yoga (I'm taking yoga out of its spiritual context here, and only referring to the physical practice of moving through a sequence of purposeful poses), then you are starting off with concentration and focus. Moving through different positions will force you to become more aware of your body, your breath, your emotions and your energy. Generally speaking, we can typically only hold three things in our mind at the same time. So if you're thinking about your left foot stepping backwards, and inhaling as you reach your arms forwards, then you're probably not thinking about your email inbox, or what you're going to make for dinner that night. As you start to breathe more deeply and mindfully, you are helping your body wake up by increasing the oxygen flow to your muscles and your brain. Remember that two-way street, the feedback loop between the body and the brain? When we hold a static pose like a plank, we have to engage the core muscles, an action which is grounding and stabilising. This is your body telling your brain, *I'm calm and still and I can endure the discomfort. I'm in control.* Even when it becomes uncomfortable, you still continue, so you are enforcing the message *I can endure.* This is an incredibly empowering state of mind, and this sense of control, this feeling of calm, will undoubtedly carry through to the rest of your day. So the next time you find yourself being pulled along by someone else's pace, to meet their priorities or their schedule, you don't have to rush or feel overwhelmed. Remember that you are in control, and you can choose to remain calm and still.

The second type of movement is strength training, and more specifically weight lifting. I know so many people, including many women, who absolutely love the feeling they get from lifting heavy weights. This kind of activity often encourages us to embody a different version of ourselves, and some even describe it as an alter-ego effect. I'd like to highlight this point specifically for women, because many of us grow up with a preconceived notion of what being 'feminine' means – and it usually has to do with power. We've been told that women are the weaker sex, that we have less power because we live in a man's world. Lifting and moving heavy weights – or doing bodyweight strength-training exercises that require you to physically support yourself – is your body telling your mind: *I am strong. I am powerful. I can lift myself up.* This is the proprioceptive feedback in action. Regardless of your gender, starting your day with weight lifting or strength training will set you up to feel strong and powerful – both physically and emotionally. When you strengthen your body, you strengthen your mind.

Finally, I want to talk about my morning drug of choice: running. We were born to run. When I take my son to school, I stand at the edge of the playground and watch the kids chase each other. Most of their games involve running, because for a child, it's a completely natural movement. I believe that when you're running through a park, or across a city bridge or along a towpath, your body's forward motion is declaring to your brain: *I am free. I have a purpose and I'm moving towards it. I am taking action.* I don't know how to choose the words to describe what running is to me, or how to do justice to my experience of it and the impact it has had on my life. Often, I lace up before a run feeling tired and stressed, but that forward movement, together with the repetition of my breath and the almost meditative beat of my feet striking the ground, brings a feeling of invincibility. My worries don't seem so big anymore. I'm awake and I can think clearly. I have more energy and anything seems possible. When I run early in the morning, the streets are quiet and undisturbed. If I time it right, I start my run in the dark, and then gradually the sky begins to change as the sun starts rising. I run the last mile back to my house against the backdrop of a multicoloured sky. Often, it only lasts for a few minutes. But this transience reinforces the importance of time and intensifies my desire to live with a sense of urgency. The sunrise doesn't wait for you – if you're late, you will miss it. Once it's gone, it's gone. Yes, there is always another chance tomorrow, but tomorrow isn't guaranteed.

Look out for how your movement and your body language changes throughout the day. Ever notice how when you feel angry or frustrated, your muscles tense up, your breathing becomes shallow, and you might clench your fists or cross your arms? Or how, when you feel happy, calm and relaxed, your breath is slower and deeper, and your muscles are relaxed? Imagine how your body and posture changes when you're sitting in traffic on a motorway and you know that you're going to be late. You're inching closer and closer to the steering wheel, gripping it tightly as you clench your jaw and practically hold your breath. (I'm imagining a cartoon version of myself with steam coming out of my ears.) Now, compare that to how your body feels when you're driving without any time pressure, on a relaxing road trip on a long open road. You sit back in your seat, sing along to Jill Scott and daydream about the countryside pub you'll stop at for lunch. In other words, your body language and energy are always in sync.

Remember that the feedback loop works both ways. If your mood affects your movement, then your movement also affects your mood. If you want to shift your state of mind, start by moving your body. Stand up, take a deep breath, reach your arms up above your head, walk, stretch, dance – just get moving. Even if you don't immediately experience a huge mood boost, nine times out of ten you will feel better than you did before. So when you think about how you want to feel each day, one of the most important things to consider is how you move.

*

I often say that movement is a universal language. It's a way to communicate and to express ourselves without words; we dance, for example, to celebrate and connect with others. It has always been a way for us to tell stories and to express an intention or emotion. Since the dawn of time, many religious festivals have used dance as an act of worship. Around the world, different cultures have their own traditional or national dance: the famous Dragon dance in China, for example, which represents power and dignity; or the Spanish Flamenco, which is dramatic, expressive and known for its emotional intensity. Perhaps one of the most impressive ceremonial dances is the New Zealand haka, which symbolises challenge and is traditionally associated with warriors preparing for battle – and which New Zealand sports teams have made widely known around the world. And have you ever seen a baby or young child discover dance for the first time? It's beautiful (and often very entertaining) to watch them wiggle and stamp their feet as they give in to an innate urge to move their body in sync to the beat of the music. This is another example of our body's inherent desire to move, and showcases how you don't have to be a pro to benefit from dance as a form of movement.

When it comes to bonding and creating new relationships, science journalist Jason G. Goldman suggests that mirroring another person's movement – whether in dance, in sports or even in conversation – helps us to foster deeper relationships. If you think about it, dancing at parties and in groups encourages social bonding, while dancing with a loved one enhances one-to-one connection. Dance partners learn to read each other's body language and to synchronise their movements.

As a consequence of these proven benefits, dance therapy has become increasingly popular for both adults and children as a psychological treatment. It explores non-verbal communication, using a combination of movement and dance as a way of expressing and addressing psychological difficulties such as trauma, anxiety, grief and depression. Kimberley Pena is a dance movement psychotherapist – she uses dance therapy to help patients with physical disabilities or mental health conditions. When I asked her about her work, she explained that:

Dance movement psychotherapy [DMP] is the most brilliant marriage of science and art. Recent studies, looking specifically at the effectiveness of DMP, showed that when it comes to reducing symptoms of anxiety and depression, DMP is just as effective as more widely known forms of therapy such as cognitive behavioural therapy.

Taking care of your mental and your physical health are of equal importance, so if you're looking for an alternative therapy, dance and movement could be a gateway to exploring new ways of expressing yourself and observing your emotions.

*

It's not a surprise to me that, when I ask people about the key to their success, they often mention having a morning movement practice. It is intentional and, for many, non-negotiable. Serial entrepreneur and award-winning author Linzi Boyd told me: 'The first hour of the day is my golden hour and it always has been. I'll start the day with a personal training session or a Pilates class. After that, most things happen for me in the morning; it's the most amazing time of the day as I've got high energy and my brain is firing, so I can really utilise that time.' And I know many people who feel exactly the same.

One person who is guaranteed to inspire you to get moving in the morning is Richie Norton, an ex-rugby player who is now a movement coach and yoga teacher. His morning routine includes taking time to make fresh tea, lighting a candle or burning incense, meditating or journaling for roughly ten minutes – and then it's time to move. This movement could be as short as ten minutes or as long as two hours, depending on what he needs that day and what his schedule looks like, but it usually starts with yoga followed by an outdoor activity such as hiking or surfing. Richie describes this morning practice as a 'superpower'.

Life happens. Every morning might not be the same but if you can start your day with a ritual or a routine, then you can start to build from there. It allows me to get my headspace and my body into the right state. It is a really valuable tool that can have a massive impact on the rest of your day, by creating a little pocket of calm before stepping out into the world and allowing other things or people to influence your state of mind.

Creating a morning routine takes initial effort, but this effort is never wasted. Taking on a physical challenge in the morning certainly requires self-discipline and consistent work. For many people, that first step is the hardest, but over time, when your new routine becomes a normal part of your day, the effort and willpower required will decrease. You'll see and feel the benefit that this one hour has on the rest of your day, and it will get easier to keep going. Of course there are still going to be those days when it is a challenge to get up and get moving. It would be much easier and much more pleasant to stay in bed – our brains are wired to avoid discomfort – but it's important to resist the urge to remain comfortable, and instead remember that short-term discomfort will lead to long-term reward. This is why so many high performers start each day with a workout, from Tim Ferriss to Oprah Winfrey. I was once told, and now firmly believe, that successful people are successful for one reason: they do the things that they know they need to do, even when they don't feel like doing them.

We all know that actions speak louder than words. An exercise that I often share with clients and mentees is counting actions as votes, so when you take action and actually do something you say you'll do, you're essentially casting a 'Yes' vote for yourself. Let's say you want to become a morning runner. The first thing you do is buy a pair of running shoes. Newsflash: this in itself does not make you a runner. So the next thing you do is tell your housemate or spouse (or cat) that, tomorrow morning, you are going to get up and go for a run. I'm sorry to say, this does not make you a runner either. But the next morning, when you wake up and go out for a run – that action validates your claim to being a morning runner because now you are embodying the behaviour and the identity of one. That run is you casting a 'Yes' vote for yourself, proving to yourself that you are the kind of person who means what they say. On the other hand, each time you say you're going to do something but you don't actually follow through, you are casting a 'No' vote – essentially a vote of no confidence – and over time, this invisible tally chart will inform how you see yourself. I want to be clear here: this has nothing to do with proving it to anyone else, and everything to do with proving it to yourself. It's a way to give yourself proof and build confidence in yourself and your ability to take action.

I once carried a book around in my bag for over a week without reading a single page. Every time I left the house, I glanced at it in my bag, certain that I'd make a start on it during my train journey that day. Then I'd sit down on the train, scroll through emails and WhatsApp messages on my phone until I arrived at London Liverpool Street station, only to have to carry the unread book around for another day. Why was I doing this? Because my actions are deliberate and I'm always thinking about my end goal, my intention was to read more in order to become a better writer. But my mistake was thinking that simply by buying the book and carrying it around with me, I would be prompted to read more often. The reality was that after taking my son to school at 9:00am, that 45-minute train journey was valuable time, with lots of different things battling for my attention. I was choosing to spend that time on my phone, rather than focusing on my goal of becoming a better writer. My actions did not match my ambition. I was continuously casting a 'No' vote every day. Once I realised this, I decided to prioritise reading as part of my Power Hour. Three days each week, I woke up, sat up in bed, grabbed that book and read for 30 minutes before doing anything else – and, crucially, before picking up my phone. The result? I'm no longer wasting my money buying books that I don't read, and my bag is a little bit lighter too.

Cast enough 'Yes' votes, and you'll stop doubting your ability to commit to a routine. You'll stop giving up on yourself, vowing to start again next week. You will trust yourself because your actions demonstrate that you really do mean what you say. This idea of casting votes has been a powerful tool for me and I've used it many times. It has helped me to achieve many things, big and small – from stopping mindless snacking late at night, to writing this book.

*

When it comes to creating your new movement routine, the first thing you need to establish is your intention. It's crucial here that you're upfront and honest with yourself about what you want to achieve, as this is what you'll need to think about when you step out of bed in the morning. Make a commitment to yourself and remember that the effort you put in will not be wasted. This new routine is not a strict set of rules that someone else has given to you; this is a choice that you are making for yourself. If you think you're too busy to make time for yourself right now, then you probably need a Power Hour more than anyone. Ask yourself:

1. What is the *purpose* of this movement? Is it taking you closer to your goals?

2. How do you want to feel after your movement? Think back to the different types of movement, and the different ways they'll impact your mindset.

3. What works well and what needs to change with your current movement routine? It might be that you don't need to change it completely, only refine it.

4. What are your blockers? What is stopping you from creating and sticking to a morning movement practice? Be honest with yourself!

But even with all of this said, I can promise you that there will be days when you *really* don't feel like it. I'm sorry to say that I am not that friend who's going to tell you, 'Don't worry, just stay in bed today, it's only one day, do it tomorrow.' You don't need that friend. I am the one who will shove you out of bed, open the curtains, turn on some loud music and do the workout with you. But as much as I wish I could (quite literally) do this, the truth is you don't need me, or anyone else. Give yourself some credit – you've done harder things in your life than a few burpees. Just remember that when your alarm goes off. And in case you find yourself forgetting, write it down and place it somewhere that you'll see it every morning, like right next to your phone or alarm clock.

As an incentive to stick to a morning training routine, I often sign up for endurance events such as a marathon or team triathlon. Working towards a specific goal not only keeps me motivated, it also gives me an opportunity to challenge my own commitment. If your movement goal doesn't have a specific event tied to it that you can sign up for and work towards, here are some other simple tips to help you stay motivated and get moving in the morning . . .

Measure your progress.

If your exercise routine is sporadic and lacking structure, it will be much harder for you to track how far you've come. It's really important to be able to measure progress, as it shows that what you're doing is actually making a difference. A good example is strength training because it's very easy to measure improvement. It's simple: can you lift more now than you could before? Whatever your goal is, seeing clear improvements will help to motivate you.

Follow a specific training guide.

Having an exercise programme to follow takes away any decision-making, which is particularly useful at 5:30am. You can simply look at the plan and get to it. A good training programme should increase the intensity gradually over time (this is important to avoid injuries). You can't go from zero to 100 in a week. When looking for a training guide or programme, make sure that the coach is qualified and is suitable for your current fitness level. There are lots of generic workout plans and guides available online, so, if possible, ask a personal trainer to tailor a specific programme to you, or alternatively recommend a pre-existing plan.

Figure out your motives.

Are you driven by the idea of moving towards something that you want – or moving further away from something that you don't want? There are two types of competitive people: some people love to win, others hate to lose. There is no right or wrong answer, but it's good to get clear on which one you are.

Get serious about your health.

Often, people don't think about strokes, heart attacks or dementia until they are well over 50. We assume that while we're in our twenties and thirties, we have the secret weapon of youth to protect us. But the reality is that lifestyle choices – and specifically physical activity and diet – will impact your health now *and* in the future. Take a moment to think about the lifestyle you want to have in 10 or 20 years' time, and start to future-proof yourself today.

*

You may be reading this and thinking that movement just isn't really a priority for you right now. You'd like to include it in some way, sure, but it's not at the top of your list of goals. In that case, consider how you could incorporate movement into your pre-existing routine. I'd say the best place to start is with your daily commute. The average commute in London is 74 minutes a day – a total of six hours a week. A 2015 report published by the Greater London Authority outlined the varying ways that commuting affects people's wellbeing, and one of the key findings was that people who walk to work (even if only for a part of their commute) are happier than people travelling by car or train. This is due to the combination of walking (increased heart rate and breathing) and just being outside in the sunlight, and supports the idea that daily movement, especially if it's before midday, will have a positive impact on both our minds and our bodies.

You could potentially avoid rush hour altogether (and reduce your travel time) by commuting earlier, or you could reinvent your journey and 'convert the commute'. Sammi Adhami, co-founder of fitness tech company Fiit, often talks about converting his commute as a way of saving time and increasing daily activity. When training for an Ironman triathlon, he uses his commute as an opportunity to either run or cycle (and he also does this throughout the day, to and from meetings across London). His company is made up of like-minded fitness fanatics, so no one seems to mind – or even notice – if he turns up to a company meeting in trainers and a sweaty T-shirt. (And most offices now have showers and hair dryers, so you don't need to worry about breaking a sweat on your way to work.) 'Managing a busy start-up, children, endurance training and daily life mean that I have to use my time wisely. As well as converting my commute, I often use the "school run" as an actual run with my son in a running buggy and my daughter on her scooter,' he explains. 'It's only two miles, but it's an easy way to incorporate movement into my day.'

Converting your commute could save you some cash too: if, for example, you decide to ditch your £8 train journey and replace it with a 45-minute cycle each morning, you could cycle over 4,000 miles and save yourself over £2,000 – more than enough to cover the cost of a starter bike. Win-win! So, how could you convert your commute? Could you walk, run or cycle for a part – if not all – of the way to work?

*

I wrote a post for my blog a few years ago about running, in which I listed all the ways that running has impacted my life. It is one of my most-read and most-shared blog posts, and reading it back now I'm struck by how much of it remains true. If running isn't your thing, many of the lessons below can be applied to other types of movement too. I'm not here to convince you that you should try running. But just in case you are tempted, here's a few good reasons to give it a go.

It shifts my focus towards what I can do rather than what I can't.

Being able to run, or do any kind of challenging physical movement, is something that I am truly grateful for. When you witness someone you love fall ill, it becomes impossible to take your own health for granted. I know how fortunate I am to wake up each day without pain, illness or disease, and running is my way of acknowledging it. Sometimes, I run simply because

I can. When life gets busy, if I'm feeling overwhelmed with work commitments and pending deadlines, the temptation is to prioritise other things. *Do I really have time to run today?* Whenever I find myself asking this question, the answer is almost always 'yes'. If it's important to you, then you will make time, even if that means getting up 30 minutes earlier. I hope that I'm still healthy enough to be able to run races when I'm 80, but it's still important to remind myself that: 'One day I will not be able to run 10K, but *today is not that day.*'

It's a never-ending challenge.

There is no real finish line in running, or any other physical exercise (and I don't mean a race). You can never *complete* or *conquer* running. As we move towards a frictionless life – endless entertainment at the push of a button; food that comes pre-washed, pre-sliced and pre-cooked; homes and offices regulated by heating in the winter and air conditioning in the summer – giving ourselves physical challenges is more important than ever. It reminds us of what the human body is capable of, in a world that is designed to make everything as easy as possible.

It teaches me patience.

I can see how people might assume I've always been into fitness, or that I found it easy from the beginning. But the truth is, those first few runs were miserable! I would run a loop near my house that was less than two miles long, and I felt incredibly frustrated that it was so hard. I am impatient, and I wanted it to be easy. But I kept running – three or four times each week – and eventually that two-mile route got easier. Unlike most things in life, initial progress with running will be linear, and you'll improve based on the time you put in. That's not to say that it won't take time, and any 'quick fixes' should be viewed with a healthy dose of scepticism. As a result, running continues to teach me patience. I try my best to accept that not everything will fit into my ideal timeline or schedule. You can't rush progress; sometimes it just takes as long as it takes.

It gives me confidence.

I don't believe that confidence is something that you are born with, but rather something that can be cultivated. Running has shown me that if I work hard, if I stick to the plan and put the (proverbial) miles in, then I can achieve whatever it is I set out to do. I've seen other people's confidence grow as a result of exercising, and I've watched that confidence seep into every single area of their lives. Perhaps it is simply knowing that you can do something today that you couldn't do yesterday. It's a visible reminder that *you can do hard things*.

It calms my mind and stimulates creativity.

I'm sure I can't be alone in having some of my best ideas when I'm out running. Maybe it's because it's one of the only times of the day when I am completely alone. (Through my own doing, I hasten to add. I love being around people – I always have.) Every once in a while, I'll go out for a tech-free run, with no podcast, no playlist and no watch to track my stats. Before I started writing this book, I would sometimes think about what I wanted to share, and I'd come in after a run and record a voice note straight away or write a page of notes that would later form the basis of a chapter. In a world full of distractions, being able to have your mind focus on one thing is a rare superpower. I'm by no means a Zen master, but running alone, without any distractions, is a mindful practice for me.

It has taught me how to fail, and how to carry on.

One of the biggest failures of my life so far was the 2018 Berlin Marathon, which I was unable to finish. It's the only race that I have ever started where I didn't cross the finish line. I spent the entire summer of 2018 preparing for this race, doing everything I was supposed to. I meticulously created a 20-week training plan. I did the long, slow training runs, the speedy interval runs and the treadmill sessions. I ran up and down the mountains in France before breakfast each day while on holiday. I even ran on the beach in Mexico in 30-degree heat to avoid missing a week of training. I have never trained so consistently for a race before. Everything was going great, until one morning I stepped out of bed and felt a sharp pain in the sole of my right foot. It was so painful I couldn't put my foot flat on the floor. But to be honest, I wasn't too concerned – surely it's normal to expect a few aches and pains while training so rigorously, right? I assumed that after a few days it would be gone, but it got worse. I started icing it every day (I'm still unsure whether this was a good or bad thing to do) and I went to see my physiotherapist, who told me to completely rest my foot until the race, if I'd even be able to run it. I was gutted – I'd worked so hard for months – but I did as I was told.

Fast-forward to race day, and as I stood at the start line the nerves kicked in. I thought that my foot would no doubt be hurting by the end, but I did not for one second imagine that I wouldn't be able to finish the race. By the time I reached 16km, the pain was constant. Looking back, I know this is the point that I should have stopped. But instead of listening to my body, I let my ego take over. I put my headphones in and turned the music up. I reached the 25km sign, but the pain was now unbearable. I was running on my toes because it hurt too much to put my heel down. That's when I had to stop. Angry and frustrated, I limped over to the medic station and watched as hundreds of runners ran past. I saw a lovely doctor who strapped up my foot to stop any more swelling, and gave me a strip of painkillers and the address for a clinic where I could go to collect a set of crutches. When I eventually made my way back to my hotel, I was exhausted and feeling very sorry for myself. To make matters worse, the hotel was full of pro athletes, press and media. There were celebration banners and balloons everywhere.

I knew that all of my friends would be out celebrating, while I'd be icing my foot alone in my hotel room. I seriously considered changing my flight booking just so I could go home.

I shared this whole experience from start to finish on social media, though I was initially embarrassed to tell people I hadn't finished the race. I'm always the one encouraging others to dig deep and persevere, and I'd had so many people reaching out and saying how following my training had inspired them to take up running or to sign up for a race. I felt like a fraud and a failure. But you know what? It turns out people really don't care if you cross that finish line or not. I realised in that moment that the only person that can put negative pressure on you is yourself. Making a mistake, or getting injured, or failing at something is always a possibility when you dare to leap. The important thing is not letting the sense of failure blind you from what those mistakes can teach you or stop you from trying again. I am proud that I showed up at the start line that day and that I raced as hard as I could, knowing that I gave it everything that I had. Injury or not, anything can happen on race day. Running a marathon takes courage.

I've done it before and I know that I will do it again. I'm grateful that running taught me a lesson in how to fail.

Lastly, it gives me a sense of freedom.

You can run whenever and wherever you want to, free from distractions, work, stress, noise; free from your responsibilities as a parent, partner, boss or fun friend. It's normal to love being all of those things, and yet simultaneously feel weighed down by the expectations of others. You should never feel guilty for craving solitude or for carving out time for yourself each day.

When I first started running, I didn't realise how much I needed that time on my own, even if it was just 20 minutes each day. My son was a year old, and as most new parents will understand, those first few months were a whirlwind. Here is a tiny person attached to you day and night – and before you know it, you're used to eating dinner with one hand, or taking a 30-second shower while singing along to 'Baby Shark' *(doo doo doo doo)*, or juggling two bags, your phone, a keep cup and said tiny person every time you leave the house.

It was also around then that my husband had become seriously ill. When I was 19 weeks pregnant, he had a spontaneous brain haemorrhage without any known reason or cause. He had a seizure that caused him to fall out of bed and onto our bedroom floor. I stood over him in a momentary state of shock, before grabbing my phone to call an ambulance. As a result of that night, he developed epilepsy and was unable to work while he tested a number of different anti-seizure medications. It was terrifying for both of us. No one could tell us if it would happen again. Our whole world had changed in an instant, and I was becoming increasingly overwhelmed and anxious. I'd started taking sleeping tablets, but I would still lie awake at night fearing that he would have an epileptic fit. Every now and then, his seizures would start again, and we'd both feel as though we were reliving a nightmare.

I'm not going to say that running was the revelation that changed my life overnight. I didn't grab my running shoes and watch as all of my problems disappeared. Life is not a Nike advert. However, when I look back at that time now, I can see how much I needed those 20-minute runs. Some days, I felt like I wanted to escape my life and quite literally run away from it all. Going for a run on my own gave me the time I needed to be free from my catastrophising thoughts, free from the fear and the responsibility, if only for 20 minutes. We all need an element of freedom. Exercise is a great place to start.

*

The important thing is to figure out which movement practice makes you feel good. If you've always thought of exercise as a punishment or a chore, try to shift your perspective. Instead, think about all the ways your body and mind will benefit from incorporating an exercise routine into your daily life. The blunt truth is that if you want to have more energy and vitality, you need to move more. If you want to improve the quality of your sleep, you need to move more. If you want to improve your self-esteem and self-confidence, you need to make a commitment and show yourself that you can follow through. Starting your day with movement will give you a sense of achievement and it will create momentum for the rest of the day. Don't just take my word for it – try it for yourself and I promise you'll see that daily morning movement is a game changer.

If you want to get real about making your goals happen, you have to get real about sleep.

The Power of Sleep

'So you want me to start getting up an hour earlier. But what about *sleep*?' This is usually the very first question I get asked whenever I introduce someone to the concept of the Power Hour, but getting up an hour earlier each day doesn't mean you have to forego sleep. We spend roughly one-third of our entire life sleeping, and it's absolutely essential for optimum health. The more I read and learn about sleep, the more I try to prioritise it – and you should too.

Putting sleep first can often seem easier said than done. The modern world just isn't set up to help us optimise sleep, and in fact it can sometimes feel like it's actively working *against* us. There are a variety of factors that influence our ability to sleep, as well as the quality of that sleep. We have 24/7 global communication, meaning you can connect with a friend online who lives on the other side of the world, no matter what time of day or night. If you live in London and work for an international company, it's common practice to stay up until 1:00am replying to emails and joining virtual meetings with the company's LA team. (I have a number of friends whose companies expect them to be online for 18 hours most days.) Many of us now have jobs that require shift work and/or round-the-clock communication. And even if you're not working until the early hours, then there are literally thousands of other reasons to stay up late. Netflix and YouTube both provide an endless buffet of temptation; there is always another new post or notification on Instagram; and I'm pretty sure there are a few WhatsApp group messages still awaiting your response. When you add these late-night distractions to a host of other factors – a diet that is high in sugar and caffeine, a lack of exercise, very little time spent outdoors, stress and anxiety, artificial lighting and a varying daily schedule – it's no wonder we're a society of sleep-deprived zombies.

For many of us, sleep can appear a luxury and not a necessity. Our society encourages us to wear exhaustion like a badge of honour, as though we are somehow more committed or hard-working if we choose work over sleep. This hustle culture encourages young wannabe entrepreneurs to work hard, play hard and then work some more. With side hustles and multi-hyphenate careers becoming a standard path, it's not uncommon for young people to finish their nine-to-five and immediately start on their five-to-nine. As for modern parents, they are now attempting to raise children while simultaneously managing a career. Once they're past the early years, sleepless nights, potty training and phonics lessons, their evenings consist of video conference calls, cheering on the sidelines of a sports pitch, helping with maths homework and attempting to cook homemade gluten-free, dairy-free, nut-free pesto pasta. Many of my friends put their kids to bed and then return to the laptop for a few more hours of work before finally collapsing into bed. Meanwhile, our own parents are up all night playing word games on Facebook and looking at photos of their neighbour's cat! Seriously, does anyone actually sleep anymore?

*

I first started taking my sleep routine seriously after reading Matthew Walker's international bestseller,

Why We Sleep. In it, Walker explains why sleep is one of the most important aspects of living a long and healthy life, and argues that modern society continues to neglect sleep – with devastating consequences. Before this book, I didn't truly understand that sleep has just as much, if not more, of an impact on our health as diet and exercise do. Insufficient sleep has strong causal links to every major disease in the developed world, including Alzheimer's, cancer, obesity and diabetes. To be honest, some of the stats in that book will shock you (they certainly scared me). For instance, Walker reveals that 'routinely sleeping less than six or seven hours a night demolishes your immune system, more than doubling your risk of cancer.' And that: 'Adults forty-five years or older who sleep fewer than six hours a night are 200 per cent more likely to have a heart attack or stroke during their lifetime, as compared with those sleeping seven to eight hours a night.' After reading the first chapter, I was tempted to put the book down at 4:00pm and go straight to bed. There are a lot of books I frequently recommend, but this is one which should be mandatory reading for anyone wanting to improve their health. It goes against the stereotypical narrative that the world's most successful CEOs manage to operate with as little as four or five hours' sleep each night. 'Short sleepers', as they are described, will often brag about how little sleep they need while labelling the rest of us 'lazy' or 'weak'. Though I'm broadly open-to testing things out myself, for now I'll heed Walker's advice: short sleep is one habit I will *not* be adopting.

When it comes to daily habits that impact high performance, sleep is by far the most critical. One of my all-time favourite episodes of the podcast is with Olympic long jumper Jazmin Sawyers. Jazmin has an incredible work ethic, even though she described herself as being 'naturally lazy' (to this day, I still do not believe her). When I interviewed her, she told me:

Sleep has been my secret weapon. I always track my sleep and the week that I jumped my personal best was after the best week of sleep I've ever had. Nothing else had changed: my training regime in the run-up to that competition was the same. Sleep was the key . . . Sleep is way more important than we think because we get so used to functioning with less sleep and we think it's fine, until you have a prolonged period getting the amount of sleep that you actually need, and then all of a sudden, wow! Your life's different.

The key takeaway? Sleep to win!

I first met The Sleep Scientist, Dr Sophie Bostock, backstage at a wellness event in 2019. Sophie and I had both been invited to speak on a panel about sleep and how to create an effective morning routine. Sophie studied psychobiology, which is the science of how our biological systems and our behaviour interact. Psychobiologists research how what we are thinking and feeling connects with our physiology, in order to better understand the human experience. As well as being up to speed on the most recent scientific studies on sleep, Sophie is incredibly passionate about helping people understand the data in order to recognise the importance of sleep. 'Sleep underpins everything. It impacts our mood, cognitive function, our ability to concentrate and recall memories, and even the strength of our immune system,' she told me. 'It is foundational for good health, and if you have a good basis for sleep then you are in the best position to live well.'

So why is sleep so critical? What's really going on when we sleep? While not all functions of sleep are fully understood, there are three key processes that take place while we sleep which have been proven to be essential for our overall health. Without them, our bodies simply cannot function correctly.

The first is the process by which our bodies repair and grow new cells: muscle repair and tissue growth all take place while we sleep, which is why it is so important to make sure that you're getting sufficient sleep when you are exercising regularly. (Especially if you're training for an endurance event or in-corporating strength or weight training into your workout routine.) Without enough sleep, your body won't be able to repair and recover fully, meaning your fitness progress will be slower and you'll be more likely to develop an injury.

The second function of sleep is to maintain the health of our brain. If you're consistently sleep-deprived, both brain function and brain health are significantly reduced. The body is incredibly complex and most of the time, if we are in good health, we are blissfully unaware of what's going on in there. It's only when something goes wrong that we notice it at all. While we sleep, we consolidate our memories and store new information that we have learned that day, for instance. Additionally, we need sleep so that the brain's glymphatic system can clear out waste products and fluids from the central nervous system that have built up throughout the day. This allows the brain to function well when we wake up. Not getting enough sleep, especially if it's for a prolonged time, will have a negative impact on our ability to make decisions, concentrate and focus. Feeling foggy-headed when trying to remember your shopping list or a computer login password might be annoying, but sleep deprivation can become dangerous and even cause serious accidents. In the UK, 20 per cent of highway accidents and up to one-quarter of fatal and serious road accidents are caused by driver fatigue.

The third function of sleep is to support our emotional well being. Sleep helps to regulate the hormones responsible for appetite and mood, and a lack of sleep disrupts the functions that control emotional responses. The amygdala is the part of our brain that is in charge of our 'fight or flight' response, and being overly tired can cause the amygdala to become overactive, heightening stress and anxiety. You'll understand the feeling well if you've ever felt irritable and overly sensitive when not getting enough sleep. You suddenly find yourself crying over something trivial that you'd usually brush off. When our ability to cope with life's inevitable daily stresses feels close to zero, often it's a signal that we need more rest.

In short, your current sleep routine (or lack thereof) is undoubtedly impacting both your physical and your mental health, for better or for worse.

*

When it comes to figuring out how much sleep you need, and how and when you're going to get it, there are a lot of factors to consider. It's become common knowledge that an adult should aim for an average of eight hours a night. 'The consensus among sleep experts is that the recommended number of hours' sleep for adults is between seven and nine hours each night,' Sophie told me. 'There are some people that have short sleeping genes and therefore require less sleep, but we think that is fewer than one per cent of the population, so it's pretty unlikely that you are one of those people.'

To gauge if you're getting enough sleep, try answering the following questions:

> ▶ Do you wake up most days feeling rested and refreshed?
>
> ▶ Do you frequently wake up before your alarm?
>
> ▶ Do you wake up at roughly the same time during the week and at the weekend?

And now ask yourself:

> ▶ Do you usually drink coffee within one hour of waking up?
>
> ▶ Can you fall asleep easily on a train or bus journey to or from work?
>
> ▶ Do you sleep in for two or more hours at the weekend?

If you answered 'no' to the first set of questions and 'yes' to the second set, chances are you're probably not getting enough sleep. Or maybe you're sleeping for a long time but the quality of your sleep is poor, and so you still wake up feeling tired. Alternatively, if usually you're able to fall asleep easily at night, wake up feeling refreshed most days, and you're not relying on caffeine and sugar to wake you up throughout the day, then you're probably getting enough sleep. For some people that might mean they need seven hours each night; others might need eight or nine.

If you've established that you're not getting enough sleep, you need to figure out what's currently stopping you. There are always going to be 24 hours in a day, so why do we often think we're suddenly going to have more time tomorrow or next Thursday? Just like all other commitments in your life, if sleep is important to you, you have to prioritise it. Admittedly, this isn't always easy, especially because during times of high stress – when we most need good quality sleep – we find it hard to switch off or calm the mind and actually fall asleep. It can be particularly hard to do so when you're under pressure and working hard towards a deadline. It's easy to think that staying up late to complete work is more important than those extra hours in bed, but it's been widely proven that sleep will help you to do better work more efficiently. We need rest in order to perform at our best.

It's also common to sleep poorly the night before an important event such as a test or an interview; ironically, knowing that we need to get a good night's sleep makes us feel stressed, and we end up looking at the clock every hour until it's time to get up. It's very frustrating when this happens, but just remind yourself that one or two nights of poor sleep isn't the end of the world; maintaining a good, regular sleep pattern is what's most important.

Sophie recommends keeping a sleep journal for a few weeks to record how much sleep you're getting each night and how you feel the next day as a result. After a few weeks, you should start to see a general pattern, and you'll probably see a clear correlation between your sleep and your mood and energy levels. A sleep journal is a good way to get an overall picture of your current routine, but try not to stress about the details.

Most people only start to analyse their sleep pattern when they're not sleeping well. And the jury's out when it comes to sleep-tracking technology – most smartwatches and health apps that offer sleep tracking are arguably not very accurate. In a recent sleep study, researchers warned that sleep-tracking tech could provide inaccurate data, and even worsen symptoms of insomnia by causing people to obsess over the results. If you're already worried about not getting enough sleep, wearing a sleep-tracking device all night, and then looking at a graph on your phone each morning that tells you that you woke up seven times, is unlikely to help you improve your sleep. Often, it only makes it harder to rest properly. Generally speaking, I think it's much better to keep a journal based on your own assessment of energy levels and mood, rather than relying on a device. Sleep routines are likely to change throughout the seasons and there will always be natural variations in our body's sleep pattern – based on daylight hours, room temperature and, for people who menstruate, even where you are in your monthly cycle – so don't let worrying about sleep be something that keeps you awake.

But wait, what about new parents? This might all sound well and good if you don't have a small human demanding 24/7 attention without a single care in the world for *your* ideal sleeping routine. Sleep is a hot topic for many knackered parents (whoever coined the phrase 'sleeping like a baby' was surely having a laugh). The first few months after having a baby may feel like you're taking part in a human torture experiment via intentional sleep deprivation, with your new baby as the grand master. 'Why does my baby hate me?' my friend once jokingly asked me. 'Is she trying to kill me? Doesn't she know that I would literally do anything for six hours of sleep right now?' But, jokes aside, taking care of a baby is tough already, and when you add in six months of sleepless nights, it really takes its toll. Establishing a good sleep routine for babies and children is critical if you want to sleep yourself. Long stretches of poor sleep can have a negative impact on your mood and health, but Sophie says not to worry straight away. 'We are designed to be able to cope with temporary sleep challenges, and there is a lot of natural variation in sleep,' she reassured me. 'Don't panic if your sleep is disrupted for a few weeks or months, but it is important to return to a good sleep routine when you can. If you're trying to establish good sleep habits for your kids, many of the same principles apply. Factors such as diet, daily activity, exposure to blue light from smartphones and screens will all impact your child's ability to sleep.' To this day, the best purchase I ever made as a parent was a £40 Gro-Anywhere blackout blind. I now get this as a gift for all of my friends as soon as I find out that they're pregnant. Sure, teddies and baby clothes are cute – but I am giving them the gift of sleep. Trust me, you'll thank me later.

So, if your kids are keeping you up all night, take solace in the fact that it won't last forever. It might be trite to say, but really the best advice is to just try to get as much sleep as you can. What are the things that you can control? Maybe you don't think that going to bed 40 minutes earlier will make much difference, but that's an extra four hours of sleep each week. Could you alternate the night shift with your partner? Can you nap when the kids do? Figure out what works best for you for now (and in the meantime, avoid operating any heavy machinery).

While it's common for new parents to engage in a battle for sleep, there is also another universal sleep war going on: a battle of the sexes. Yes, that's right, in a world that was created by men, for men, the gender gap continues after dark too. I'm sure you're aware of the gender pay gap (women will typically earn 17 per cent less than their male colleagues), but did you know that women also lose out on sleep in a similar way? This may be due to a number of different reasons, such as women traditionally taking on more of the emotional and domestic labour of family life, and the fact that sleep is impacted by biological differences too. Throughout her lifetime, a woman may miss out on sleep as a result of hormonal changes, breast feeding, period pains, and cold sweats due to menopause, for instance, and in a recent UK survey, many women attributed a lack of sleep to their partners snoring.

It's worth considering what you can do to address both short-term and long-term sleep issues as soon as possible. Ladies, make sure you are getting the sleep that you deserve.

*

You've probably heard the terms 'night owl' and 'early bird'. Most people – especially when they're faced with getting up at 5:00am – will declare themselves to be night owls, but how do you really know? When I spoke to Dr Zoe Williams, an NHS GP and television presenter, we discussed the difference between the two. 'It's down to our genetics. It's called your chronotype, and it tends to run in the family – for example, all of my family are night owls,' she explained. 'Genetically, we are all predisposed to either one or the other, early bird or night owl. What this means is that if you're not someone who is physiologically designed to function in that way, it can be quite difficult to be up and at work before 9:00am, because the first half of your day is when your body naturally still wants to rest.' You might be thinking, *Aha that's me, I'm a night owl for sure!*, but it's important to consider the lifestyle factors that might be tricking you into thinking you're a night owl. Just because you've been staying up late for years doesn't necessarily mean that you're a natural night owl: your lifestyle and social calendar might be dictating your sleep schedule more than your genes.

Here are some signals that can help you figure out your real chronotype:

> ► Early birds tend to have a big appetite in the morning, whereas night owls are more likely to skip breakfast.
>
> ► Early birds can do focused work such as writing in the morning, but night owls will do their best work in the evening and can easily work into the early hours. Night owls will happily eat dinner after 8:00pm.
>
> ► Early birds prefer to exercise before midday.

It will come as no surprise to you that I would describe myself as an early bird. Most days, I'm up before 5:30am and I'm at my best during the first half of the day, but this hasn't always been the case. Back when I was a dancer, I was performing in a West End musical every night for almost two years. The evening shows would start at 7:30pm and finish at 10:15pm. It was a high-intensity rock show and the energy on stage was wild! When I left the theatre at the end of the night, my blood pumping with adrenaline after performing to a crowd of over 2,000 people, I'd walk to Holborn station, buy a sandwich and some chocolate, and read a book on the journey home as a way to switch off and calm down. I'd arrive home at 11:30pm, still wide awake, and I'd often continue singing in the shower until midnight. My work dictated my lifestyle for years, and I guess back then I would have thought of myself as a night owl. So, am I naturally an early bird or have I just got used to this new morning routine?

I asked Zoe if it is possible to change your circadian rhythm and to train your body to switch from one to the other. The body's circadian rhythm, also known as the sleep/wake cycle, is like a 24-hour internal clock. It cycles between sleepiness and alertness at regular intervals. Her answer was that 'You can change your sleep pattern, but you will still be predisposed to one more than the other, so once you reset and establish a new routine, you have to make sure you're consistent or you'll easily slip back into your old pattern again.' If you're going to set your alarm clock an hour earlier, then my top tip is to focus on going to bed an hour earlier too. It might seem like an obvious point, but you'd be surprised how many people don't do this and complain that getting out of bed in the morning is impossible. When I first started waking up early for my Power Hour, I found that going to bed earlier was the biggest challenge. For me, it takes more willpower to put my phone down and sleep than it does to get up in the morning and go for a run. Avoiding the temptation to scroll through memes for another ten minutes requires ninja-like self-discipline. Once you nail your bedtime routine, then trust me, getting up is the easy part. Commit to a one-week trial and get into bed one hour earlier than you usually do for the next seven days. If you stick to it consistently, by day eight you'll probably wake up before your alarm and be feeling ready to take on anything. Don't underestimate the impact one relatively small change can make. No ifs or buts; it's just one hour.

*

Hopefully, by now we are all in agreement that sleep is important. Knowing that is the first step, but what are you going to do about it? I've already outlined a number of things that could sabotage a good sleep routine, but there are also some positive changes you can start to implement straight away. (And on that note: put this book down *now* if it's past your bedtime! Resume reading tomorrow morning when you're rested and can pay full attention – this next part is important.)

Here are three things you can do to optimise your sleep routine and wake up feeling ready to take on the Power Hour:

1. Create a calm and relaxing space to sleep.

Your bedroom should be a place that is quiet and free from distractions. Try to avoid clutter and mess in your room, and if possible avoid letting your work follow you into the bedroom. It's hard to switch off at the end of the day if you can still see visual reminders of your work projects, to-do lists, invoice statements and so on.

Invest in some low-watt lightbulbs or a lamp for your bedroom, and avoid bright lights after 8:00pm. Once you're asleep, the room should be as dark as possible, as sleeping with even a small amount of light exposure impacts the quality of your sleep. The National Sleep Foundation recommends that we should: 'Shield artificial light properly in the bedroom (by turning your alarm so that the light faces away from you, for example), and use light at night only when it's absolutely needed.' I've made my bedroom as dark as possible by investing in blackout blinds and making sure it's a tech-free space. Once I turn out the light, I can barely see my hand in front of my face. Admittedly, this takes a bit of time to get used to, but it means that I sleep most nights for seven or eight hours without waking. Whenever I travel, I always place a piece of paper or a book in front of the hotel alarm-clock light, and I unplug the TV to remove that annoying red LED light. If you can't make your room dark enough, then maybe consider wearing an eye mask instead.

Add plants to your bedroom to evoke a sense of calm and tranquillity. Plants not only enhance the room's design, they can also improve your sleep. Some plants, such as ivy, are naturally air-purifying. Ivy is usually an outdoor plant, but when brought indoors it can drastically reduce the airborne mould in a room in just a few hours – great for allergy sufferers. I have ivy plants in my bedroom and my bathroom, and they are low-maintenance and pretty resilient (the goldfish of houseplants). Other plants such as the snake plant (sansevieria) will produce oxygen at night, which is considered to help promote sleep. Similarly, placing a lavender plant next to your bed, so you can inhale its calming scent, has been shown to reduce your blood pressure and heart rate. Personally, I use a deep-sleep pillow spray most nights before I go to bed. It's great for travelling too: no matter where I am in the world, as soon as I spray it I'm reminded of my own bed. I recognise the smell, and associate it with sleep. It may be a placebo, but either way it smells good – so what's the harm?

Once you've created a dreamy sleep haven, eliminate tech from your bedroom as much as possible. No TVs, laptops or phones allowed! Order an alarm clock online today for less than £10, instead of using your phone. (You can thank me later.) Tech is most people's biggest bedtime distraction, and the blue light emitted by screens will stimulate the same part of the brain as the midday sun. Studies show that blue light impacts our brain function for up to 90 minutes after we stop looking at a screen. So if you're still looking at your laptop at 11:00pm, you won't be able to sleep deeply until the early hours of the morning. Wearing blue-light blocking glasses is an easy way to reduce the harmful effects of tech on our eyes, brain and sleep.

Lastly, invest in the best-quality mattress you can afford. Many mattress companies now offer 90-day sleep trials, so don't be afraid to be picky. It might sound boring, but finding a great mattress is like finding a great hairdresser: it's worth putting in the extra time, and you'll just know when you've found the right one.

2. Eat well, sleep well.

What you eat, when you eat and *how* you eat will all have a significant impact on your sleep pattern and energy levels. Diet trends and health headlines seem to change every week; the varying advice can be overwhelming and it's difficult to sort out the facts from the fads. Far too often the focus is placed solely on weight management or weight loss – but there's a lot more to diet and nutrition than that. For instance, eating high-sugar processed foods throughout the day can cause dramatic spikes in blood sugar. We experience a peak followed by a crash of energy, and if you then reach for a cup of coffee or more sugar to help stimulate you, the same pattern continues again, confusing the body. Calories aside, this constant change in blood sugar means that even if you are getting enough sleep at night, you may still be feeling tired throughout the day. Broadly speaking, a diet that promotes good sleep is similar to a diet that promotes good health. It needs to include a variety of carbs, proteins, fats and fibre, and be low in processed foods and alcohol.

Which foods could help you to sleep? You might be surprised to learn that some foods naturally contain a hormone called melatonin, which makes your body feel sleepy. A diet with plenty of eggs, fish, almonds and cherries, for instance, could really help you get a good night's sleep. And foods that are high in potassium and magnesium – natural muscle relaxants – can improve sleep too. (Bananas are a good source of both.) You may have heard that drinking a cup of warm milk before bed will help you sleep. But is it the milk or is it the ritual of a comforting hot drink that really makes the difference? (It's important to bear in mind that many of the largest food studies carried out in the last decade have been funded by the dairy industry.) A study has shown that: 'Scientifically, there may be some link between the tryptophan and melatonin content of milk and improved sleep. But perhaps more powerful is the psychological link between warm milk and bedtime as a child. Just like hot tea, a warm drink of milk can provide the perfect soothing backdrop for a relaxing bedtime routine.' My favourite bedtime drink is either a rooibos tea (naturally caffeine-free) or a decaf chai made with oat milk.

Eating a large meal close to bedtime can interfere with the body's processes as it prepares for sleep. For this reason, author and physician Dr Rangan Chatterjee suggests eating your last meal three hours before you go to bed. Ideally, you shouldn't go to bed feeling hungry, but allow yourself time to rest and digest before you go to sleep. Sure, there will be times when eating late can't be avoided – social events and holidays, for instance – but if you can create a routine at home that allows you to eat dinner by 7:00pm, it could help to improve the quality of your sleep.

If you're going to bed early in an attempt to get more sleep, but you're lying in bed feeling alert and awake, then reducing or even removing caffeine from your diet could be a good place to start. Caffeine (the world's most popular drug) is a stimulant that can enhance cognitive function and concentration, and boost your mood. Whether it comes from drinking coffee or caffeinated energy drinks, many people claim that they *need* a caffeine fix to feel alert and awake in the morning, and they also use caffeine to boost their energy later in the day. Similarly to other drugs, if you drink caffeine daily, over time you will increase your tolerance and need a higher amount of caffeine to achieve the same results. Although you might not consider drinking two flat whites each day an addiction, broadly speaking an addiction is simply something that you need on a regular basis or you'll have clear physical withdrawal symptoms. If you typically drink two or more cups of coffee each day and you suddenly stop, initially you're likely to experience headaches, low mood and difficulty concentrating: in other words, withdrawal symptoms.

When it comes to sleep and caffeine, the effects will vary from person to person. The trouble is that for many people who sleep poorly, they reach for a coffee or energy drink as a result of feeling tired during the day, but this may lead to more poor sleep. It's a negative cycle that is easy to fall into and difficult to disrupt. That is why Sophie advises us to consume caffeine before midday. Caffeine can stay in your system for 6 to 12 hours, so if you're drinking caffeine in the afternoon, it's going to have a negative impact on your sleep. If you decide to cut down on caffeine, consider switching to decaf instead of eliminating it all together (remember page 90, on replacing non-useful habits).

3. Get outside in daylight.

Being outside in natural light during the day will help to regulate your circadian rhythm, which is controlled by a part of the brain called the hypothalamus. External factors, like daylight and darkness, send signals to the hypothalamus that tell us it's time to sleep or wake up. This is why Sophie suggests going outside in daylight every day before midday, because it's a surefire way to put your body into waking mode. If you don't incorporate some outside time into your Power Hour, then consider cycling to work or taking a walk around the park during your lunch break. At the very least, open your curtains and let the light in first thing in the morning, and try to avoid lazing around in bed in the dark (even on weekends). If you're getting up before sunrise during winter months, consider using a dawn-simulating alarm such as a Lumie clock. They are designed to emulate sunrise and sunset, by gradually increasing or decreasing a brightening light. A few guests on the podcast, such as Venetia Falconer and Annie Clarke, have recommended them as a Power Hour essential. Exposure to natural light will increase the brain's alertness during the day, which in turn will also help you sleep better at night.

At the end of the day, when it starts to get dark, the brain signals to the body to release melatonin. This process can easily be disrupted by jet lag, shift work or late-night Netflix binges. Since we all live in homes with electricity, it's very easy to have the lights on right up until the moment that we go to bed. Bright light in the evening will confuse your body's internal rhythm, meaning that you might find it hard to fall asleep when you get into bed, despite feeling really tired. As an experiment, try turning off all electric lights at 9:00pm and light a candle instead. You'll probably be yawning and ready to fall asleep within an hour.

*

What if you're already doing everything right? No tech in the bedroom, early-morning workouts, you've switched to decaf, your room is dark and filled with plants – but you're still lying in bed unable to sleep because your mind is busy. Some nights, it feels like the moment your head hits the pillow, you're suddenly more alert than ever. When that internal dialogue starts, it can be difficult to switch off and sleep. Mine usually goes something like: *Today was a good day. I need to remember to reply to Natalie's message tomorrow. Oh, and I forgot to email Jess to tell her that I've sent the slides as a PDF. What day is it? Tuesday. I can't wait to see Ayeisha on Thursday, I wonder if she's booked a table. It'll be busy, we should book. This bed is so comfy. Shit! Is Jude's swimming lesson at 5:00 or 5:30 tomorrow? I should check. Okay, go to sleep. I've still got so much work to do before Friday. Don't worry about it now, get some sleep. But wait! Now would be a really good time to think about Brexit, or climate change. Go. To. Sleep.*

Sound familiar? Nights like this are why I now keep a notebook underneath my bed. I just purge all of my thoughts and questions onto the page, then shut the book. This helps for two reasons: firstly, I know that I won't forget anything important, as I've written it down, so I *allow* myself to forget about it and relax. Secondly, the process of writing it down often makes me *feel* tired – I'll literally start yawning within minutes. Mission accomplished.

Often, the reason we feel like our mind is racing at night is because we've been so busy during the day, going from one thing to another, that we haven't taken time to process all of our thoughts. When I talk to high performers about their daily routines, nine times out of ten they tell me they have some kind of mindfulness practice – this could be meditation, breathwork or journaling. But they all agree that there's no quick fix or hack when it comes to mastering mindfulness: it requires patience and time. Personally speaking, I've never really committed to meditation, and you know what, I'm okay with that. I've been told so many times by so many different people, 'Adrienne, you *have* to learn to meditate. It's so important. You of all people need to meditate,' that I sometimes feel like a rebellious child being told off by my more enlightened friends. In these instances, my get-out-of-jail-free card has been breathwork.

Breathwork has really changed the game for me, and the more I learn about it, the more I want to practise. If you're not familiar with breathwork, let me break it down. Essentially, breathwork is a practice that requires you to consciously alter your breathing pattern. This could be as simple as inhaling and exhaling in a consistent rhythm for a few minutes, or it can be a more forceful breath pattern that dramatically increases the amount of oxygen in the body. Breathwork takes a bit of time to get used to, but in my experience the benefits are instant. I've done breathwork classes and workshops, and I've even done one-on-one breathwork therapy with Richie Bostock, known as 'The Breath Guy' and the author of *Exhale*.

Breathwork pioneer Wim Hof, known as 'The Iceman', is a Dutch extreme athlete and world record holder who created and made popular his own breathwork practice – the Wim Hof Method. He has personally demonstrated incredible, sometimes unbelievable, feats using what he calls 'the power of the breath'. He holds records for swimming underneath ice while holding his breath, has completed barefoot half-marathons across ice and snow, and has been the subject of multiple medical experiments. Using breathing techniques, Wim has shown medical doctors he can do things that were previously thought to be impossible. And he can teach others to do them too. Science journalist and author of *Breath: The New Science of a Lost Art*, James Nestor, says, 'We are only just scratching the surface of what is possible when it comes to breathwork and human potential.' The benefits of regular practice include: increased immunity, emotional healing of past pain and trauma, enhanced self-awareness and reduced feelings of stress. I can't recommend breathwork enough, but don't just take my word for it. Do some research and try it for yourself.

If you are too stressed out to sleep, then developing a mindfulness practice is a great tool for stress management. The reason I say stress 'management' is because that's what we need to do: manage it. It's unrealistic to suggest that we should simply try to *avoid* stress – we can't eliminate stress entirely from our lives.

We have been told time and time again that stress is bad for us, that stress causes ageing and chronic illness and disease, but surely, hearing all of that just makes us feel even more stressed! Health psychologist Kelly McGonigal says that we need to understand our own stress mindset. She explains that although experiencing stress can have some negative impact, the way in which we *perceive* stress can be just as detrimental. By constantly telling yourself that your life is stressful, and by believing that stress is exclusively bad, you are conditioning your mind and body to act as though you are suffering. But if you believe that you will in some way benefit as a result of stress, you allow the high-pressure situation to be a catalyst for action. Do you believe that stress is debilitating and hindering your progress? Or do you believe that stress increases your resilience and your ability to problem-solve? We all know people who say that they work better under pressure. The added stress of a deadline spurs them on to produce superior work more quickly.

Kelly says that people who try to avoid stress because they believe it's harmful are statistically more likely to get divorced and less likely to be promoted at work. By avoiding stress or confrontation with your partner, you will dodge difficult but very important conversations. This only leads to unhappiness (and greater stress) later on. In a similar way, if you're trying to please everyone to avoid stress at work, you're more likely to go along with the group consensus and less likely to volunteer to lead projects or take on more responsibility. Putting yourself under pressure or getting out of your comfort zone may be stressful – but it's not all bad.

Another way of thinking about stress is this: typically, we are only stressed or bothered about things we care about. Being stressed means that you have things that you value in your life. I often challenge myself to think in this way: *Adrienne, you're* lucky *to have these problems.* What I'm saying here is that having a mortgage and bills might be stressful, but it means I have a nice house to live in. Feeling stressed about how I'm going to manage my time and social commitments means there are many people who want to spend their time with me – another good problem to have. I'm not suggesting that all of life's problems are simply blessings in disguise, but when I'm trying to fall asleep at night and have all of these things keeping me awake, I prefer to view my list of stresses in this way, and to feel grateful that I have so many things to care so deeply about.

*

The truth is that the modern world will continue to demand more of our time and energy. It will continue to offer new and shiny distractions that appear way more fun and exciting than sleep – but that is not an excuse. We are human, and we have not evolved at the same pace as technology. Our body's processes have remained the same for hundreds of thousands of years. Whether we like it or not, we need to sleep and we cannot expect to perform at our best if we're constantly running on empty.

Everyone wants to feel good! And it is undeniable that our mood and energy levels are directly linked to sleep. Sleep well and you're much more likely to feel and live well. How can you create a life that you love, and then actually *live it*, if you're exhausted all the time? If you want to get real about making your goals happen, you have to get real about sleep.

If I want to learn from someone, I will watch what they do before I listen to what they say.

The Power of People

The Spartan Ultra is a 30-mile-long foot race that includes 60 obstacles along the way. There is a strict cut-off time for participants to complete the course, and so many who take part in the race do not make it across the finish line. The obstacles vary in difficulty and require a combination of skill, strength and endurance to complete. The race course changes each year and challenges even the most hardened athletes to push themselves beyond their limits.

What's most interesting to me about this race is that it is virtually impossible to complete the course alone. Many of the obstacles require you to join forces with others in order to make it on to the next one. Imagine that you're ten miles into the race, it's cold, wet and muddy, your body is starting to fatigue – and you're only a third of the way there. You're standing at the bottom of an eight-foot wooden inverted wall, and the only way to conquer it is to work with other racers to lift each other up. Let's say you team up with two other people who form a strong base together, and then you *literally* climb to stand on their shoulders and reach the top of the wall. Once you grab hold of the top and pull yourself up, you don't just say, 'Thanks, see you later,' and continue without looking back. You turn back, and you pull up those who helped you. Forming a team is the only way to win.

The Spartan race is a great metaphor for life. Yes, we all need motivation and encouragement from time to time, but we also need people who will support us practically. There are some goals you simply will not be able to achieve on your own. Figure out what they are and be willing to ask for help. What strengths are you missing? Who do you know who can help you climb that wall? Think of the people who have been there before you and know what you're trying to achieve. And once you get over that hurdle, always remember to turn back and look for the next person coming up behind you. Make sure you pull them up too.

Tribe, community, network, team – whatever you call it, our survival as a species has always been dependent on our ability to live in cooperation with others. Over the last few years, I have become increasingly aware of the power of relationships and networks. I'm not just talking about career and business networking – I'm talking about friendships and personal relationships too. I've seen the importance of collaborating with others, the value of seeking help from role models and mentors, and how we in turn influence and lead others. I've learned (sometimes the hard way) that some relationships will give you more energy than they take and some people will naturally bring out the best in you, while others will consistently challenge you. We are all impacted greatly by the people in our lives, for better or for worse. Recognising this is the first step in harnessing the power of people.

*

Humans are ill-equipped to live alone, and being isolated from others has dramatic negative effects on our health. When I interviewed scientist and journalist Marta Zaraska during the Covid-19 pandemic, we discussed the psychological and emotional impact of social isolation, and how being isolated from others is the single most detrimental thing to human health, above a bad diet and lack of sleep and exercise.

What I've learned through researching diet, exercise and psychology, is that there is a much bigger picture. Some things are very simple, but very important. Our social connections, the way we live and interact, and our mental attitude are actually more important to health than many of the other factors that we typically focus on, including diet and exercise.

Living in communities means we subconsciously adhere to a sort of social contract, acting and behaving in ways deemed to be socially acceptable by the group. This impacts everything from the way we dress, to the way we talk and think, and even the way we move. For example, you probably wouldn't wear your pyjamas to work, listen to your music loudly on an aeroplane without wearing headphones, or knowingly walk around with spinach in your front teeth. Like it or not, conformity is part of human nature. Our DNA *wants* us to be the same as others, so that we can belong to the group and therefore survive; in prehistoric times, being kicked out of the tribe was literally a death sentence. And although this is no longer the case, we still care deeply about our role within a group dynamic. The modern world now celebrates individuality and uniqueness, but many of us still fundamentally crave acceptance from the tribe, especially when we're young. Even in the playground there is a social hierarchy and we very quickly try to figure out our own role within it: one child takes the spot of 'top dog' or 'alpha', and the others follow in a sort of unspoken ranking. Children as young as four display behaviour that demonstrates allyship to their peers.

Which tribe you belong to also has a massive impact on your circumstances and prospects. This is why parents care so much about who their child is friends with at school: they know the influence a peer group can have on their little angel, which is why they want their child to be surrounded by positive role models or, at the very least, to hang out with those kids they consider to be inherently 'good'. As we grow up, social influence and conformity apply to most areas of our lives, from tiny daily habits to life-changing behaviours. For example, if your friends are always late to meet you, you probably won't worry about turning up late to meet them – it's clearly an acceptable behaviour within your group. If all of your team members are vegetarians, when you all go out for dinner after work, you're less likely to order a steak even if you're not vegetarian yourself. Social influence has the potential to impact you in far more significant ways too, from how much money you earn, to how likely you are to own your home, and even how many children you have.

We all know the phrase 'birds of a feather flock together', but what I am most interested to know is this: what comes first, the chicken or the egg? Perhaps the reason so many of my friends are runners is because *I* am interested in running. Or am I interested in running *because* many of my friends are runners? Both are true to an extent. We exist within a circle of influence, and what we see others demonstrate as routine or 'normal' will dictate what we view as normal too. When lots of my friends are training for a race, it automatically makes me want to sign up as well; if they can fit in training alongside their work and family lives, then surely I can too. And I know I'm going to feel left out when race weekend comes around and they're all on their way to the airport to catch a flight to Barcelona. Damn FOMO!

In reality, most people will belong to more than one tribe at once. When we're young, friendships can be fickle and we're very easily segregated into groups: the sporty ones, the cool kids, the academic high-achievers. And while it might not be as pronounced as the *Mean Girls* cafeteria, there's some truth behind the fiction. This subconscious selection is often heavily influenced by our personal interests, culture and proximity, and this can shape our identity as we proceed into adulthood. Even as we leave some of those labels behind, we inherit new ones: the mums, the runners, the entrepreneurs. Today, I belong to many different friendship groups and I play different roles within them, so while each identity is an authentic part of me, each group requires me to show up in a different way. I probably don't interact with my work colleagues in the same way that I do with my old school friends. In other words, our energy and behaviour may change depending on the relationship we have with the group, and our role within it.

Due to the nature of my work, I met lots of my friends online via social media, and I now have genuine friendships that never would have happened if it weren't for the internet. That might have been a strange thing for someone to say a decade ago, but it's becoming far more common as social media continues to influence the way we interact with one another. At the same time, I'm proud to say I have some friends that I've known for almost 20 years – from school days to weddings, having kids, losing parents and changing careers. Navigating and sustaining adult friendships isn't always an easy thing to do, but throughout the inevitable highs and lows of life, some friendships can stand the test of time. Having said this, not all friendships will last, and some people aren't meant to stay in your life as you change and grow. Maybe your lives have gone in very different directions over the years, and now the things you used to share are gone. I was 22 years old when I became a mum, and while all of my girlfriends were incredibly supportive, I quickly established a very different bond with my mummy mates because we were all sharing a life-changing experience at the exact same time. (Mum WhatsApp groups really are the fourth emergency service: from weaning recipes to post-baby sex, there's nothing you won't be able to find an answer to. Everything and anything goes!) The chat was hilarious, supportive and, at times, heartbreakingly honest. You will never forget some friendships, even if they only last for a season of your life.

I guess friendships are just like every other relationship: some are simple, some are complicated and some should have ended a long time ago. Some friends stay in our lives because of a shared history, past circumstances or a feeling of obligation, and when this happens, you will often find yourself resenting the relationship. Your interactions start to feel like hard work. Those are the friends who always seem to find a way to criticise you or to question your decisions, as though you owe them an explanation. (PSA: You don't.) It's a hard thing to do, but sometimes you have to recognise that it's time to move on and essentially break up with a friend.

Energy is contagious. We've all been around those people that are so energetic and fun that they lift the energy of the entire group. It's like walking into a piano shop, sitting down at a grand piano and pressing down on the middle key – when you do so, the middle string of every other piano in the shop starts to vibrate too. This phenomenon is known as 'sympathetic resonance'. (How much do you want to go to a piano shop and test out this theory right now? Trust me, it works.) But I'm sure you've also been around people who instantly drain the energy of the group: mood-hoovers that suck up all the vibe. Your energy will do one of three things upon meeting another person's: it will attract, repel or resonate.

Don't get me wrong, I'm not suggesting that we just cancel anyone who doesn't agree with us, or who challenges us. I don't want to live inside an echo chamber. But I believe there are some fundamental friendship non-negotiables: friends should love and support you in the pursuit of your goals; and they should be compassionate, no matter how big or small your problems may seem. They should celebrate your successes and share in your joy, and most importantly, they should encourage you to be yourself! It goes without saying that I value honesty, but we all know those people who think being honest is giving you their unsolicited advice in a way that is destructive rather than constructive. Newsflash: it's not radical candour and it's not being 'real' – it's just rude. When a friendship continually drains you or makes you feel bad about yourself, something has to change. There are very few people who enjoy confrontation, but if you need to break up with a toxic friend, remember that *you can do hard things*. If you don't do anything about it, what you allow will continue.

Relationships go both ways: just as those in your social circle influence you, you will also influence those in your social circle. Leading by example is the most powerful and effective way to influence others. Actions speak louder than words: there's a reason people say 'show, don't tell'. If you want your partner, your kids

or your parents to start exercising more and eating
healthier foods, you'll find it a lot easier to convince
them by leading by example rather than dictating a
strict regime. If you're showing them that walking,
cycling and running are enjoyable things to do – rather
than a punishment that they must endure on their
own – they're more likely to join you. This is especially
true for young children. By cooking healthy meals and
eating together, you can educate your whole family and
introduce them to foods that they've never tried before.
In other words, you can't ask your kids to eat their
greens if they never see you doing the same. Personally,
if I want to learn from someone, I will watch what they
do before I listen to what they *say*. Are they disciplined?
Are they hard-working? Are they kind? An instruction
is good; an example is better.

It's important to consider the impact of your social
circles when you're working towards your goals and
attempting to create a life that you love. How are the
words and actions of other people in your life influencing
you? Are you surrounded by people who encourage you
to pursue your goals? Do they share a similar mindset,
values and work ethic? Are they demonstrating habits

and behaviours you want to embody yourself? And are you doing the same for them?

Although some of my friends might have very different lifestyles and interests, we typically share many of the same core values. For instance, many of my friends understand personal ambition and are goal-oriented: they're studying or creating their own business, training for a triathlon, and so on. As I've been writing this book over the course of the last six months, at times I've had to be completely immersed in it, and had to dedicate all of my energy and focus solely towards this one project. As a result, I have been less available for friends and family than I would usually be. But because they share a similar work ethic and ambition, they've been very understanding and, crucially, they're not trying to tempt me away from my laptop to hang out with them. There's none of that 'Come on, it's just one night! Why can't you work on the book next week?' They get it. They understand my mission. They see that this is a season in which I am socially hibernating in order to create this book. Rather than making me feel guilty for not being available, they're cheering me on because they know how important this is to me.

If you're working hard towards a goal, you may have to make temporary adjustments to your life and to your schedule. Make sure you communicate this to the people in your life and let them know just how important it is to you. However big or small the goal is, having support from like-minded people will undoubtedly aid your pursuit, as they understand the process. That said, you can't blame others for holding you back if you don't choose to prioritise and focus. You have to clearly outline the goal, manage others' expectations – and then get to work.

*

Many of my projects initially require me to take action in order to drive the idea from a concept to something concrete, but once any project gets started, the only way to build and expand on it is to find a team to help you. I know there are times when I need to be the one to steer the ship, but often I also need to ask someone else for guidance and help in order for me to move closer to my goals. You can do anything, but you can't do everything. Collaboration is key.

It's important to realise from the outset, however, that different personalities work differently, and you have to be mindful of that in order to make the most of each other's skills and play to your individual strengths. Psychologist and author Adam Grant talks about collaboration and the dynamics of a successful team in his 2018 TED talk, saying, 'You need humility. Humility is having the self-awareness to know what you're good at, and what you're not good at.' He also reveals that 'studies show that when you have humility in a team, people are more likely to play to their strengths. Instead of going for the spotlight, they take on the roles needed to help the team win. You don't have to be the best player to add real value.'

I'd definitely describe myself as a team player. If I'm on your team, I'm going all-in for you. Being a team player doesn't mean always leading or always following: it's about being able to do both, depending on what the situation asks for. Reflecting on this has made me realise the importance of being *adaptable*. Grant explains that not everyone in the team can be an A player; you have to have Bs and Cs too in order for the team to perform at its best. Being a B or C player doesn't mean that you're not as important, or that you're simply there to support the 'All Star'; each role is critical for a team to function and succeed, and the best teams have a mixed group of skills and a variety of roles. What role do you typically take on within a group? Do you find yourself naturally gravitating towards a leadership role? Or are you more often the supporter? Are you a good mediator and negotiator?

In my experience, getting friends on board to help you can be brilliant. All relationships need trust and it's absolutely critical that you trust the people you're working with. You'll need to be able to lean on them when making important decisions and know that they are dependable. Over the years, I've become friends with lots of people in similar industries to mine: many of my friends have completed marathons, written books or host their own podcasts. We're always leveraging each other's insights, support and advice. If a friend asks me for training advice because he's trying to run a 10K personal best, I'm happy to help (and will often be cheering for him at the finish line). Similarly, I've reached out to two of my writer friends on multiple occasions during the process of writing this book, to ask them for practical advice. Their input is invaluable because they've been there and done it before. If you find asking for help difficult, remember that most people are happy to lend a hand because the reality is that someone else's success does not diminish your own. In fact, the wisest people know that you'll gain just as much from being a teacher as you will from being a student. Right, Mr Miyagi?

I know what it's like to continuously have to compete with your peers. Back in 2010, I was busy auditioning for dance jobs in musicals – and anyone who's ever been in the performing arts will know the aggressively competitive environment, the everyone-out-for-themselves atmosphere. You turn up to an audition, queue up outside with hundreds of other hopefuls and are given a number so nobody has to bother learning your name. You step into the room to compete for the job, with all of the other candidates standing beside you, and after each round the panel sends people home. By the end of the day, you exhaustedly look around to assess the remaining few. It's not quite *The Hunger Games*, but not far off either. You have to be resilient if you're going to have a career as a dancer, and accept that competition is just a part of the job. If you're working in any ultra-competitive industry, it's inevitable that you are going to experience both highs and lows, so it's important to create a support team around you. Sometimes you'll need a shoulder to cry on; other times you'll need a kick up the ass. Ideally you'll find someone who can do both.

Steve Sims, author of *Bluefishing: The Art of Making Things Happen*, is someone who knows everything there is to know about the power of networks and social influence. As well as being featured in *Forbes* and the *Sunday Times*, Steve has delivered speeches at the Pentagon and Harvard University (not bad for a man who dropped out of school at 15 to begin working as a bricklayer in east London). As an entrepreneur and CEO of the luxury concierge service Bluefish, he built his entire business around his ability to network and create relationships. 'If you get your friends together and you tell them, *I'm going to do X – I'm gonna start a podcast or I'm starting my own T-shirt company* – you're going to get a bunch of different responses,' he explains. 'You'll get some saying "Go for it!" You might get some people saying, "Well, how are you gonna do that?"

Now, that's not negative, that's them challenging your commitment. It's important to be challenged because it refines your thought process and your commitment. People can spot things and think of things that maybe you're too close to see.' He goes on to describe that not every challenger is well intentioned: 'But every now and then you'll get one mate that'll say, "Ha, you can't do that." That person that sits in the corner and mocks you for trying. They do not want you to succeed, because they believe that it will demonstrate that they can't.'

Look at your current group of friends: how many people are likely to give you a response similar to the first two, and how many will be similar to the latter? Most importantly, which kind of friend are *you*?

Consider the following: you've been offered a job that requires you to relocate to another country. It's a great job, you've always wanted to live abroad, and now you have the chance. The downside is that you don't currently have any friends or family in that country, and your partner's work requires them to stay here. Oh, and the offer is a three-year contract. Who do you ask for advice? When a start-up company is facing an important decision, they will often meet with their board of directors for guidance. Typically, the board is made up of investors, who have something to gain if the company succeeds and something to lose if the company fails. When it comes to making an important decision in your own life, why not assemble a board of directors for support? Each person needs to be invested in some way: in other words, they have to want to see you succeed.

So, who's on your board?

Family / partner: These are people who care about you, and most of all want you to be happy. They are also the people who will be most directly impacted by your decision.

Manager / boss / agent: These are professional connections who want you to succeed in your career. They may benefit financially from your decision.

Mentor: This is the person (or persons) who wants you to grow and develop personally. They understand your values and what motivates you.

Someone much younger than you: In addition to those listed above, you should also seek out someone who is significantly younger than you. They are important, as they will have a different worldview to yours and can offer a different perspective.

Someone much older than you: This is an obvious one – they've been around longer, seen more and potentially done more than you. Listen to their experience, wisdom and advice.

Financial advisor / lawyer: They can give impartial, practical advice and offer important information that you may not know enough about. (For instance, foreign tax rules, visa costs, the small print in contracts . . .)

Give your board members as much relevant information as you can and then discuss the various outcomes, both good and bad. You may receive conflicting advice and you might not always get the feedback that you want to hear. The point is to gather insight and knowledge from people you respect and trust, but ultimately you'll have to trust yourself as the final decision will always be yours: it's your life after all.

*

How do you go about building your board and finding the right people to surround yourself with? When I interviewed award-winning businesswoman and entrepreneur Aicha McKenzie, I asked her for her advice on creating a powerful network. Aicha's agencies manage talent, models and dancers, and work with fashion brands such as Burberry and Dior. On top of that, she also choreographs and creates performances for events such as the MTV music awards, the Grammys and the Olympics opening ceremony. She has worked with some of the world's biggest superstars – from Kanye West to Victoria Beckham. Both the fashion and the music industry are notoriously cut-throat, so I was keen to hear what she had to say about how to navigate professional connections.

We don't like the word "networking", because it kind of implies that you want something. I think the focus should be on building authentic relationships and friendships. You can't successfully "network" if you're just looking to take something; there's got to be an exchange, like any relationship. Every person that you encounter throughout your entire journey is important. Being nice to everybody is a quality that you need to embody – not just being nice to the people who you think can help you out, or help you get to the next step on the ladder.

We've all seen the person who is desperately scanning the room trying to figure out who the most important people are. They start a conversation with you, only to zone out seconds later once they deduce that you're of little value to them. Don't be that guy/gal.

Aicha also advised taking a long-term view when building meaningful relationships at work, and not underestimating the people who are already in your life.

Remember that your peers are your networking circle and you're all growing together. You may be at a very junior level right now, maybe you're interning, maybe your friend is working in a different industry, and another friend might be more entrepreneurial, while someone who you went to school with is over there doing that thing –

that's *your* circle, and it will grow and grow. Fast-forward, and you realise that you've all grown together: that friend is now an editor, another friend is now a head of their department – and then, yes, now you have a highly influential circle of connected people who you socialise and work with. It's got to be based in real relationships and not just, *Let me be over here with these people because I'm trying to get something out of it.*

Realising that you *already* have a network, one with lots of potential, and investing in the relationships and friendships that you already have is brilliant advice – and it's a great place to start.

However, sometimes your existing circle might be limited. This could be due to your background, your location or your socio-economic status. Regardless of the reason you want or need to reach out to new people to establish a wider network, there are a number of ways to do it. The most obvious option is to reach out to people online – this is the easiest (and potentially laziest) route to take, but also a really effective one. I've learned so much from authors, athletes and business coaches just by interacting with them online. The internet allows us to message pretty much anyone in the world now – but it's also a very crowded party, so don't take it personally if you never receive a response, and don't let it stop you from trying someone else. If you find yourself struggling to know how to reach out to someone digitally, here are some tips I've gathered over the years:

Do:

▶ Choose the right form of communication. For business opportunities, use LinkedIn, email and Twitter. On Facebook, only use pages or groups and avoid messaging people via their personal profile pages. For everything else, there's Instagram.

▶ Get a mutual friend to digitally introduce you, via email if possible.

▶ Make sure your message is concise and to the point. No one has time to read your life story before you ask them for a favour.

- Do your research. It shows that you're serious and you've done some groundwork.

- Be honest and humble. People value honesty and can easily tell if someone is being disingenuous.

Don't:

- Start a message to a person you've never met with 'Hey babe'. Ever.

- Message people on multiple platforms at the same time. I once received a Tweet from a journalist, asking me to reply to her earlier email. Not cool.

- Sign off with 'I look forward to your response' or 'Thanks in advance' (or anything similar). It's a real turn-off for me: it feels presumptuous and implies a sense of urgency to reply.

- Write a template email and then copy and paste it to multiple people without at the

> very least personalising the name. It's lazy
> and annoying.
>
> ▶ Be afraid to follow up with a second email if
>   you don't hear back, but I'd probably leave it
>   a week before doing so.

It goes without saying that you're far more likely to broaden your network if you're consistently meeting new people, so if you'd rather meet people face-to-face, attending workshops and events that are relevant to your industry is another simple option. Here is some advice I've found useful over the years:

> ▶ Avoid the urge to invite a friend to go along
>   with you. I know having someone you
>   know with you might make the experience
>   more comfortable, but being with a friend
>   makes you less approachable, and you'll just
>   spend the whole night chatting to your mate

rather than being forced to talk to anyone
new. Invite your friend for a glass of wine
afterwards instead!

▶ Once you're at the event, don't try to 'work
the room'. You don't have to meet every
single person or be the centre of attention.

▶ Avoid small talk: try to ask interesting
questions and then *really listen* to people's
responses.

▶ Always be very intentional about learning
and remembering people's names. It's a small
thing but it makes a big difference, especially
if you're following up the next day on social
media or email. A top tip for remembering
names when meeting new people is to repeat
the person's name back to them immediately
after they say it. For example:

'Hi, I'm Ally.'

'Hi Ally, I'm Adrienne, great to meet you.'

This sounds obvious – but trust me, people always seem to appreciate it. If you meet someone and you don't instantly recognise their name and you think you may mispronounce it, simply ask them to repeat it. It's far better than saying their name wrong over and over again. (This has happened to me multiple times and it is very annoying.)

I'm naturally an extrovert, so I will talk to anyone, but if you're an introvert it doesn't mean you're not good at meeting new people. If the thought of introducing yourself to strangers at a busy industry event makes you feel nauseous, I'd recommend reading Susan Cain's *Quiet: The Power of Introverts in a World That Can't Stop Talking*. The book outlines the differences in the brain chemistry of introverts and extroverts, and she suggests tools to help introverts better understand themselves and their strengths. You don't have to be naturally loud or chatty to create a network of impactful relationships; you just have to figure out which situations you're most suited to.

A good tip is to ask each of your friends to introduce you to one new person who they think you'd get on well with. Similarly, if you're starting a new business, podcast, event, and so on, ask each of your friends to share it with one friend who they know is interested in that area. Then ask if you can return the favour: connecting people is always fun and you never know what one introduction could do.

If you're in a position of influence, ask yourself how you can become a connector. Who could you introduce from one group to another? Do you know someone who is just starting out in a new career and could do with some support? How about your friend who's just had a baby and doesn't know many other new parents? Start sharing your contacts and connecting people and you'll not only help them to grow their network, you'll also become a social linchpin.

Podcast host Jordan Harbinger teaches a six-minute-networking course online that shows you how to reach out to new people and how to stay connected to your network. He says that creating an influential network of like-minded people is essential for success in any career, and he also advises us to 'dig the well before you're thirsty'. In other words, don't wait until you need a network of people to begin assembling one.

*

No one's path to success is linear. Whatever goal you're working towards, there will no doubt be hurdles and unexpected challenges, so it's a good idea to seek mentorship from someone who can guide and support you along the way. When I interviewed my own mentor, Ben Wharfe, on the podcast, I asked him to explain what mentorship actually *is* and how to find a good mentor.

Imagine that you could speak to an older version of yourself and ask that future you for advice – questions like, what were the biggest challenges they faced and how did they overcome them. Now imagine you could have an ongoing relationship with that older self, and how great an impact it would have on your decision-making and your development. Essentially, that's what mentoring is. As a mentor, you're taking all of

the skills and knowledge you've learned over
the years – the battle scars you have as a result
of your previous experiences and failures –
and figuring out how they can help the person
you're mentoring achieve their goals. The aim of
mentoring is to help the mentee discover more
of who they already are, not to make them more
like you,' he stated. 'It's important to understand
what mentoring is and to set it up right – it's
not about just having a nice chat or someone
offloading all of their problems and complaints
on you.

If you're considering searching for or becoming a
mentor, Ben had some practical advice on how you
can make the most of that relationship.

One of the key things that you need from every
single conversation is tangible actions. The mentor
should give one or two things that the mentee can
go away and work on. It might be recommending
a book to read or suggesting a person that they

should reach out to. You might give them an exercise to complete on their own. When they later come back to you and report back on the action they've taken, firstly they are developing, but secondly you're building a relationship of trust and showcasing that *I am giving up my time for you*. The mentee, in turn, is showing the mentor that they are willing to do the work and that they value the advice and the time given to them.

I find that last point particularly important to highlight. I've mentored people, and it's been mostly a positive experience. I've mentored women of different ages, in different industries and at different stages in their career. I do my best to give them honest advice, try to challenge their thinking and encourage them to develop their own understanding of a situation in order to make better decisions. The feedback that I've received from all of them is that, just by meeting me once each month, they are more motivated to take action because of the feeling of accountability that comes with it. The only time the process didn't go so well was when the woman I was mentoring kept trying to imitate me: in the things I do, say, eat and even wear. It very quickly became clear to me that she wasn't trying to develop her *own* thinking in order to become a better version of herself. Instead, she thought that emulating me would lead her down the same path and to the same outcomes. Of course, I was flattered at first, but I felt uncomfortable with the weight of the responsibility. She would ask me for advice, but it felt like what she *really* wanted was for me to make the decision for her. This is an easy trap to fall into, and if you are seeking mentorship (or if you are mentoring someone) you need to set out clear expectations from the start, and make sure that both of you are aligned on what the boundaries of the relationship are.

So what about those who claim to have done it all solo? Those people who created something from nothing, all on their lonesome. What does it really mean to be 'self-made'? It's a term used to describe someone who has succeeded in life without any help or assistance from others, and while I understand the concept, I don't believe it is possible for someone to be fully self-made. Not everyone has a mentor, but nobody exists in this world alone: it is impossible to go through life without being influenced by others (unless you were born, miraculously alone, in a cave you never left – in which case you're probably not reading this book). This influence could be good or bad, big or small, but it is *there* nonetheless, whether you acknowledge it or not. You will have been influenced by people you've seen on TV, faces you've seen on the covers of magazines, and by family members in your house, kids in your class, teachers, bosses, friends, fans and critics. Even that teacher who told me 'Don't get your hopes up' unknowingly played an indirect part in my success. So is anybody really self-made?

When a person such as Bill Gates is described as a 'self-made billionaire', it gives all of the credit and glory to the individual. In Bill Gates's case, for instance, it does not acknowledge that he had access to top education (he attended – and dropped out of – Harvard) or that he grew up as part of the wealthiest 1 per cent of Americans. I can't believe that having access to high-achieving and well-connected people had no part to play in his ascent to success, or that it didn't influence everything from his decision-making to his willingness to take risks. Of course, we need to give credit where credit is due – and Bill Gates has achieved a long list of extraordinary things – but let's not discount the people that these 'self-made millionaires' have encountered along the way.

*

We're all unique, and we each have our differences, but what's interesting to me are the things we all share. We all love, we all cry, we all feel anger and envy and joy and hope. No matter who you are, where you live or how much money you have, we will all experience illness, and one day, we will all experience death.

I like to think that we are all in this together – not in a hippie kum-ba-yah kind of way, but in a very real and concrete way. We're all aligned by the things that we share. This book is about creating a life that you love, but if you're trying to do it all on your own, then the pursuit will be less enjoyable and a lot less meaningful. Who is going to help you to create your life? Who do you want to spend it with? Who else will benefit as a result?

We cannot live this life alone. The good news is you get to choose the people that you want to spend it with.

Your actions have to match your ambition.

The Power of Purpose

Where to begin? I have so much to say about purpose, and even the word itself carries a lot of expectation and pressure. We feel the need to identify our 'life's purpose' because we believe this is a way to validate our identity. We place too much emphasis on what we *do,* and confuse it with who we *are.* Often, we believe we have to embody the stereotypical characteristics of a role: for example, if you're a medical doctor, then there's an expectation that you'll also be knowledgeable, trustworthy and compassionate. If you're a lawyer, you're viewed as being confident, ambitious and diligent. An artist is creative and sensitive. The big problem is that when we don't subscribe to a clearly defined role, or don't fall into a 'category', we can be left feeling lost. And even if you do feel like you fit into a neat box, most likely you will change in many different ways throughout your life, so how can you remain tied to the idea of a single, static 'life's purpose'?

Many self-development gurus will tell you to 'find your purpose' or 'follow your passion' with the intention of motivating you to pursue something of meaning and value, but when you're feeling stuck and uninspired, this well-intentioned message can leave you over-whelmed and confused. For some, a perceived lack of purpose can even lead to self-loathing, hopelessness and depression. On the one hand, giving someone the advice to simply 'find your purpose' is sort of clichéd and generic – as if you could just sit down with a pen and paper to brainstorm for a couple of hours and voilà! you've figured it out. But on the other hand, it's not something to dismiss completely. I believe that being clear with yourself on exactly what your purpose is and what you're passionate about will help everything else fall into place.

If I'm passionate about something, it evokes a strong emotion and a reaction. This could be good or bad; love or hate. You can instantly tell when someone is talking about a topic they're passionate about because their energy will change. They might speak with excitement and enthusiasm, or demonstrate anger and even rage. You might be incredibly passionate about big issues such as social justice and equality, or environmentalism, sustainability and climate change – but you can simultaneously be passionate about a variety of other things too, such as music, travel and art. When it comes to your work and career, I believe you must start with an area of personal interest – something that you're truly passionate about – simply because most of us will spend a huge amount of our adult life working. If you're passionate about the work that you do, you're more likely to enjoy it and to excel. If you're not, then you'll eventually start to resent it. In reality, some jobs are just a short-term means to an end and that's fine, but when it comes to creating a *career*, it's important that you enjoy what you're working on. I'm sure you've heard of the 'Sunday blues' before – the feeling you get when you're mourning the weekend and dreading the week ahead; whenever I tell people I love Mondays, I'm met with contempt (and lots of eye rolls). But just hear me out. My reason is simple: there are going to be a hell of a lot of Mondays in your life, so if you hate Mondays, that's a big chunk of your life that you hate. Life is too short to wish each week away and live solely for the weekend.

This doesn't mean that your work has to be viewed by others as exciting or 'cool' – but it has to be stimulating for *you*. Don't fall into the trap of 'compare and despair': scrolling through social media can quickly make you feel as though everyone else's careers look way more interesting and glamorous than yours, and suddenly you're doubting the satisfaction you get from your work. Remember that everything you're seeing has probably been curated for the 'gram, showing only a partial depiction of reality. Just because someone else's work *looks* exciting, it doesn't mean that it's like that all the time, and it doesn't mean that *you* would enjoy it even if it were. I know some people that hate public speaking, so presenting to a room full of people would be their worst nightmare. Those people would not enjoy my life, but *I* do – and that's the key. Avoid the urge to keep looking at what everyone else is working on and focus on the things that are interesting to you.

Compared to passion, purpose is less about emotion and preference, and more about an innate feeling of duty – towards the people you love, the planet, even yourself. I often find that 'purpose' and 'passion' are used interchangeably, when in fact they are two very distinct things. You can be passionate about a number of different things, and these will no doubt change throughout your life. On the other hand, your purpose is your *reason*, the big Why (with a capital W) you choose to do what you do. I believe the best way to get started in identifying your purpose is to establish your own unique set of values. What are the things that are most important to you? What do you *truly* value the most? Try to be as specific and honest as you can; there is no right or wrong answer. For one person, the thing they value the most might be equality and fairness. For someone else, it might be their family and everything else comes second. Another might value ownership of their time, and the freedom to create their own schedule. I want to make clear that these are not mutually exclusive – you can value all of the above, all at once, but what you need to do is highlight which one you value *the most* at this point in time.

For some of us, our values may have been established when we were very young. Maybe you grew up with little money and saw your parents struggle to pay bills and provide the basics. Perhaps you noticed that, as a result, you were unable to gain access to the opportunities available to your peers, and this has formed your opinion of money. Personally speaking, I know this was somewhat true for me. It's easy to understand why some people set out on a mission to make a lot of money. I've heard many wealthy entrepreneurs say things like: 'I grew up poor and so I decided very early on that I would never be poor again.' People often demonise this idea of wanting to 'get rich', as though it's shallow or crude, but if making money is your goal and what drives you, don't shy away from it. Do not allow others to shame you for it either – own it! Let's be real, we live in a capitalist world and we are conditioned to want more. We're told left, right and centre that we should earn more, spend more and continually strive for more. I'm pretty sure that a lot of people, if asked to answer truthfully, would say they'd like to earn more money. Wouldn't you? My question is, is money your *most important* value? It might be, and there is nothing wrong with that. But often, people don't actually want money for money's sake: they want whatever they believe money can bring them – safety, security, agency, freedom.

Once you've outlined both your passions and your purpose (remember to differentiate between the two), then you have to assess *how* and *when* you will pursue them. Unfortunately, this is not a quick and easy thing to do; it's incredibly complex and will probably take some time. As someone who likes statistics and practical solutions, I will always attempt to come up with a formula or process to calculate a solution to any problem. Imagine if it was as easy as $x + y =$ your entire life's purpose! (I'm envisioning the three sevens on a Las Vegas slot machine.) But sadly, it's far more nuanced than this. The challenging – and somewhat contradictory – feeling I have is that although your passion and purpose are not necessarily the same thing, if you have a skill or a talent that aligns the two, *that's* when you've really hit the jackpot.

*

When I look back at my school days, I find it funny that I was often scolded for talking too much. Every year, my school report said something along the lines of: 'Adrienne is an enthusiastic student and she enjoys socialising with her peers. However, she lacks focus and talks too much, and this is often distracting and disruptive to others.' It makes sense that as someone who loves to talk (apparently too much), I would later use my voice as the foundation for my career. My passion has always been people – I see myself as a professional encourager. What I do and *how* I do it may change, but my passion remains the same.

Years ago, when I was working as a personal trainer and leading group fitness classes, I learned very quickly that there were two parts to the job. Creating a 12-week programme and showing someone which exercises to do was only 50 per cent of it, and the other 50 per cent was giving my clients the energy and empowerment they needed to keep going. I had to be able to show up at 6:00am on a foggy cold morning in January, and my job was to get the best out of whoever was standing in front of me. I had to encourage them and show them that they could *do hard things*, both physically and mentally. Even now, whether I'm recording a podcast or preparing to deliver a talk, my objective hasn't changed: it's to encourage people.

I want to show up with energy and deliver a feeling. I want my words to be impactful. I want to inspire people to take action, to make a change, and to be brave enough to start that thing they've always wanted to do. I often feel as though I see people's true potential even before they do. We all have different skills, talents and superpowers: mine is the gift of encouragement. What were you told off for when you were young? Maybe it was a parent or teacher scolding you for spending too much time staring out the window, lost in your own imagination. Perhaps that creative imagination is actually your superpower.

As I gained more personal training experience, I saw time and time again that the same issues kept coming up for each of my clients. Why did they find it so hard to create new habits? Why did they give up on Friday only to start again every Monday? What were the fundamental changes they needed to make in order to achieve their goals? I knew that to become a better coach and to understand my clients, I had to piece together both the physical and the mental challenges they were facing. I started to read books about psychology, mindset and human performance.

I studied and compared different diets, read articles about sleep, and listened to podcast interviews with thought leaders such as Tim Ferriss and Jordan Harbinger about everything from biohacking to habit formation and self-improvement. Once I discovered this area of interest – my passion for helping others achieve their goals – I became a voracious learner. Identifying my passion was the crucial first step, but I also needed to give myself the tools to pursue it. The world has changed a lot in the past few decades, and we now have access to an abundance of knowledge thanks to technological innovations – there's nothing you can't find a YouTube tutorial for. You can learn a lot more than you think just by asking questions and dedicating as much time as you can to increasing your knowledge and improving your skill set. Worried that you don't have the right qualifications? Trust me, there are a lot of people who are far less qualified than you, doing the things you want to do. They are no more capable than you or I; they just have the confidence to go for it, or at the very least to try.

I'll be honest, any time you start something new, you'll probably feel overwhelmed at how little you know.

If you've ever spent five minutes on the language app Duolingo, repeating the phrase 'the girl eats the apple' in Italian eight times (*'la bambina mangia la mela'*, in case you were wondering) before getting it right, then most likely you'll be able to relate to the painfully frustrating feeling of being a beginner. But not pursuing your passion simply because you don't yet know enough about the topic is a terrible excuse. At one point in your life, you didn't know how to ride a bike – but you learned; you didn't know how to cook an egg – until you did; and once upon a time, you didn't know how to drive a car – and now you do. Why should learning computer coding be any different? Of course, there are some obvious exceptions (I really hope there isn't a brain surgeon out there somewhere who just watched a few YouTube tutorials and decided to learn on the job), but realistically, most of us could probably acquire a new skill within the next year if we were willing to commit more time to learning.

Commitment is a rare commodity and it requires dedication, but I don't think there is a single ingredient that is more important when it comes to achieving your goals. Just because you have identified an area of interest or a passion, it doesn't mean that going after it is always going to be fun. You'll need to be committed to the *process*, as well as to the final outcome. Whenever I talk about commitment, I immediately think of the Olympians I've met. I'm in awe of the sacrifices and lifestyle changes that a professional athlete has to make in order to become the very best in the world. These changes are not short-lived – they dedicate their entire lives to the pursuit of excellence. They have to be disciplined about everything, from how they train and where they live, to what they eat and how much they sleep. When I interviewed British track and field athlete Morgan Lake, I was blown away by her perspective on commitment. Morgan started her journey at just five years old, when her father was the first to spot her potential. Seven years later, she was described by *Athletics Weekly* as 'possibly the best 12-year-old athlete on the planet'. Morgan competes in the heptathlon, meaning she needs to master seven different track-and-field disciplines. Currently, she holds 23 national age-group titles and she was the youngest member of Team GB at the Rio Olympics in 2016. I asked Morgan how she managed training alongside her education, and the sacrifices she had to make in the pursuit of such great success. She explained to me that:

It was quite easy in the beginning, but it definitely got harder when I went to secondary school. I wanted to be with my friends more, and I was just with my dad the whole time as he was my coach then. I went to boarding school, and after lessons when the other kids were socialising, I'd be out training. I felt like I was missing out. I remember being 13 and telling my mum, 'I don't want to do this anymore.' She was really calm and just said, 'Okay, that's fine, you might have to drop out of school because you're there on a sports scholarship, but you can start over again.' She emptied my training kit and all of my medals onto my bed, and I knew in that moment, *Actually I don't want to quit* – and I've never questioned it since. I often think about that day, and I remind myself that really big dreams demand really big sacrifices. That's kept me going, and I know that what I want to achieve is much bigger than what I'm going to have to sacrifice to get there.

Talking to Morgan reinforced my ideas about how our actions have to match our ambition. What you do daily will establish who you become permanently. So if you've decided that your goal is to create your own business, do your actions today match this ambition? If you're buying lunch and coffee from an expensive cafe every day, but your aim is to save money for an epic travel adventure, do your actions match your ambition? If you're brutally honest with yourself and you know that your actions don't match up, maybe it's because you just don't want it badly enough; when you *truly* want something, down to the core of your bones, you'll do anything and everything to make it happen. Don't get me wrong, I'm not saying that everyone wants to, or should want to, become an Olympian, travel the world or start their own business. Your ambition is yours and yours alone. That's why it's so important to get clear on exactly what *your* goal is, what you *really* want, and then consider, *What is it going to take to make this a reality?* If you don't want to do the things required again and again, then there is only going to be one outcome. If your actions don't match your ambition, either change your actions or change your goal.

*

So what if, unlike Morgan, you didn't grow up with one specific goal? Maybe you don't yet have a clearly defined vision for yourself and your life, or know what your passions are. If you're reading this and thinking, *Adrienne, this is all well and good but I have no idea where to start*, here are some questions to help elicit a response. Answer them as honestly as you can.

> ▶ What would you write a book about even if you knew that nobody else would ever read it? *If no one besides you will ever read it, then it's not performative in any way.*

> ▶ Who do you think of when you hear the word 'successful'? *This indicates how you define success for yourself.*

> ▶ Ten years from now, what do you want to be known for? *This question shows you how you wish to be perceived by others.*

▶ What did your ten-year-old self love doing?
*Maybe part of you would still love that today,
but now your life is too complex and busy to
allow time for it.*

▶ What can you do all day and be so engaged
in that you forget to eat?
*For me, this is talking on the phone to a friend.
I can happily chat for two or more hours and
I'm completely unaware of the time passing.*

▶ If you knew that this was your last year to
live, what would you start doing right now?
*This one is very important. People don't like to
talk about death; it makes them uncomfortable.
I know it's not exactly a fun conversation-
starter, but it is important to think about
because (at least in this context) it can really
help give you perspective.*

The questions are not in any specific order and they
do not relate directly to each other – it's simply an
exercise to get you thinking. In doing so, you might

find that discovering a new passion will take you down a completely different path to the one you're currently on. It's important to allow yourself that flexibility, opening yourself up to the reality that your goals and passions will grow and develop alongside you.

*

A few years ago, I started researching and reading about plant-based diets, specifically for endurance training. This research very quickly led me to explore veganism, and I began to understand a lot more about how consuming animal-based products impacts the health of the planet, as well as the health of humans. A friend recommended that I read two books in order to further my understanding: *The China Study: The Most Comprehensive Study of Nutrition Ever Conducted*, by biochemist Thomas Colin Campbell; and *Thrive: The Vegan Nutrition Guide to Optimal Performance in Sports and Life*, by endurance athlete Brendan Brazier. After reading both of these, I was persuaded to give the vegan diet a go. Initially, I said that I'd try it out for six weeks, for no particular reason other than I thought this seemed like an adequate amount of time to be able to assess how the diet was affecting my training and overall health.

I was very quiet about it at first – I didn't want to start preaching about my newly discovered veganism before I'd given it a fair shot. At the end of my six-week trial, I was feeling pretty good. I was training hard, my energy levels were consistently high, I was recovering and sleeping well, and perhaps the biggest noticeable difference was my complexion. My skin had never looked so good, and other people started to ask me about my skincare routine and which products I was using. I came across a few initial challenges when it came to eating out and having dinner with family and friends, but overall it was going well and the pros far outweighed the cons, so I decided to continue my experiment. I ended up sticking with the plant-based diet for about two years, and my husband and son adopted it too, but I was still pretty non-committal. I used to joke to friends that I was a 'secret vegan'. Even though I was enjoying this new way of eating, I was never die hard about it. I didn't make veganism the centre of my world because, truth be told, I'm not that passionate about it. For me, it was just about fuelling my body in a way that I believed to be optimal, and if it had a positive impact on the environment and saved some animals too, then it was a win-win.

However, after about two years of eating a plant-based diet, something changed and I found myself wanting to eat meat again. For some reason, I felt kind of embarrassed and even a little ashamed to admit it. I didn't want to give in to that patronising idea that my veganism was 'just a phase'. Why do we have such an aversion to changing our mind or our opinion? It doesn't mean you're flaky or that you've given up and so therefore 'failed'. Change is good! Your interests and passions can and most probably will change throughout your life. I was curious and interested in veganism for two years, and then things changed and I moved on. Life will ebb and flow and that's normal. I care deeply about a lot of things, but that doesn't mean that I have to commit my entire life to each one of them. There are a handful of things that *will* matter for an extended period of time – maybe even your whole life – and you need to make sure you leave yourself with the energy and space to go after them. You can't fight every battle, so it's important to acknowledge that and make your peace.

About a year ago, I was out running while listening to a podcast interview with rapper and entrepreneur

Jesse Itzler. During the interview, Jesse was reflecting back on his life and talking about his philosophies, mantras and how he felt about recently turning 50. He explained that, as he celebrated his fiftieth birthday, he'd had an acute realisation about the passing years and his own mortality. He worked out that, seeing as the average life expectancy of a male living in America today is 78, he only had 28 summers left. Just let that sink in. Have you ever had words hit you like a punch to the face? I can remember exactly the road I was running on, and the overwhelming feeling I had. It gave me goosebumps. That meant only 28 more New Year celebrations and only 28 more challenges. (Jesse completes a physical challenge each year, such as an ultramarathon.) Jesse then spoke about his father, explaining that using these same stats, his dad may have fewer than ten summers. Jesse only visits him twice a year, meaning they'll only have another 20 face-to-face conversations together. I instantly did the maths to figure out how many summers I potentially have left. As I write this, I am 33 and the average life expectancy for a woman living in the UK is 81. Meaning, on average, I have 48 summers left. Of course, this number is undetermined – I could live a lot longer, sure, or maybe a lot less. The point is: it is a finite number, and I can't afford to waste a single one.

I often think about this imagined summer countdown, and it really makes me focus on how I want to spend my time. What am I currently prioritising? If I've got 48 summers left, what am I going to do to get the most out of each one? Well, I know what I'm *not* going to do, which is waste them by working 24/7 or doing things I don't really want to do due to a feeling of obligation. You know that wedding invite from that friend you haven't seen much of in the last few years? The wedding is in the South of France and it's a four-day trip, so it's going to cost you hundreds and essentially hijack your holiday fund. The kids aren't invited and you've got to ask Nanny and Grandad to move into your house while you're away. Sure, you're happy for the couple and you wish them well, but you've only met the groom a few times and you don't even know anyone else on the guestlist. Remember, this is one summer you ain't ever getting back. The lesson here: stop saying yes to things you don't really want to do in order to please others. (I get the struggle, I'm a recovering people-pleaser.)

Instead, ask yourself: How do you really want to spend those summers? Where do you want to go and who do you want to go there with? What will make those summers meaningful for you? If you're reading this, Jesse, thank you for the wake-up call. It certainly got me thinking – and more importantly, it led me to take action. After listening to that podcast episode, I created a list of 100 things to do, places to visit and people to meet, all of which are meaningful to me in some way. They can be big or small – the important thing is that they *matter*. Instead of simply writing a bucket list in a notebook somewhere and then forgetting all about it, I have my list on my phone and I look at it at least once a month, highlighting the things I plan to tick off that month. I've even added deadlines for some of them, because as soon as you add a date to a dream, it becomes a plan. Here's a few of the things on my list:

1. Live in Italy for a whole summer (minimum 3 months)

2. ~~Run the London Marathon~~

3. Give blood

4. ~~Write a book~~

5. Interview David Goggins

6. Go camping

7. Visit Vancouver, Canada

8. Get a tattoo

9. Attend the Olympics

10. Volunteer for a charity for six months

11. Learn to snowboard

12. Visit Rio de Janeiro, Brazil

13. Attend parkour lessons

14. ~~Deliver a TEDx talk~~

15. Run the NYC Marathon

16. ~~Watch a Broadway show~~

17. Get a dog

18. Go on holiday with my sister

19. Go on holiday with my brother

20. Read the entire Bible

21. Host a NYE party

One more thing: don't expect others to share your goals or even to view the world in the same way you do. Your purpose and passions are uniquely *yours*. There's nothing worse than someone trying to convert you to their way of thinking, and in my experience the best way to win over someone is to show them. Live your life in line with your purpose and others will see it. They can choose to join you or not, but do not attempt to drag them along kicking and screaming.

*

Surely, finding your purpose is not as easy as writing a list of 100 things and then ticking them off one by one? Maybe not, but it's certainly a good place to start. The problem many of us face is that our life gets in the way of us *actually* living our lives. What's stopping most people from pursuing their passion and creating a life that they love? Whenever I deliver talks or host webinars, there will usually be a Q&A at the end, and without fail the same three concerns come up, over and over again: time, money and fear.

People often tell me that they don't have time for 'soul-searching' in an attempt to discover their passions, let alone their purpose. They're too busy, and the weeks, months and years pass so quickly that there's no time for idealistic daydreaming. When it comes to work, they can't afford to take time off, and they're not sure how (or even if) it's possible to make money from their passion. Sure, going freelance or being a creative entrepreneur *sounds* cool, but can you actually earn enough to make a living? They see choosing to pursue their passion as a luxury they cannot afford. And those who are really honest might tell me that they'd love to pursue their passion, but they're terrified of taking the leap. They know what their 'dream life' looks like, but they're too afraid to go after it in case they fail.

If your issue is time, and you find yourself repeating, 'I don't have time, I'm too busy,' you need to ask yourself: too busy doing what? When did being 'busy' become our default way of living? Busyness has become a status symbol: it signifies that you are important and your time must be really valuable. That's why everybody wants it, right? If you *weren't* busy, what would that say about you? If you're not busy, then maybe you're no longer in demand, maybe you're replaceable, maybe you're not needed? But if you never have time for dinner with a friend because you're 'too busy' with work, then the harsh truth is that dinner with your friend isn't a priority – your work is. I believe time is the most valuable thing you have and the most valuable thing you can give to another person, so I really do think this same rule applies across the board. If you don't have time to work out, it's because it's *not that important to you*. Don't have time to read a book? It's not that important to you. Don't have time to visit your parents? It's not that important to you. We will always make time for the things and the people we value the most. It's not easy to admit it, but – excuses aside – the thing taking up all of your time is usually the thing you value the most.

I've spent a lot of time being 'busy' in the last few years, and trust me when I say that busyness comes at a cost. In one of my favourite poems, 'Home' by IN-Q, he writes: 'I was working for a living, but it wasn't working because I wasn't living.'

I often think about this line when I find myself 'too busy' working to do anything else. I'll admit that it's a constant struggle for me to find the right balance between work and life, so I know that it's not always easy to simply carve out *more* time. My career now allows me to blur the lines between work and life, and I often say that, because I love what I do, it doesn't really feel like work. But no matter how much you enjoy doing something, work is still work. My work is aligned with my purpose, but that doesn't mean that it's always fun or that I never need to take a break from it. When work and life become so close together, your whole world becomes your work. You wake up thinking about your to-do list, your conversations are centred around work, everything you read or watch is somehow linked to your work – who you *are* becomes what you *do*. It's very easy for your passion to become your obsession. Imagine taking two balls of Play-Doh, one red and one blue, and rolling them up together until you have one ball that looks like a marble. Now imagine trying to separate the red from the blue, or work from life. It's virtually impossible.

If your current schedule is a packed Tetris-board of working, emails, social obligations and deadlines, with an occasional night off, is it worth it? If this is only a short-term situation taking you towards a longer-term reward, then I agree that sometimes you just have to put your head down and power on. But if you feel like you are repeating the same cycle day after day, week after week, and as a result you are 'too busy' to even think about your purpose, let alone pursue it, then you have to recognise this and put the brakes on.

On reflection, this capacity to spin a lot of different plates at the same time is partially what has helped me to succeed. However, I know that in the past, the lack of separation between work and life meant that I neglected other important things. Looking back, I think many of my friendships have suffered as a result of my lifestyle choices. Sometimes, trying to align schedules with a friend is harder than trying to book a table at the most exclusive restaurant in London. Each of our calendars has a three-month waiting list and an allocated window of 90 minutes or less. The conversation might go something like:

Hey, are you free for brunch
this weekend?

> No, sorry, I'd love to catch up soon but
> I've got loads on this weekend . . .

Ah, that's a shame, haven't seen
you for ages!

> I know, it's been way too long,
> when can we get together?

The next few weeks are pretty
busy with work, how about the
start of April?

> Hmm, might be tricky, school
> Easter holidays. But I'm free on
> the 10th after 6pm?

Yes, the 10th I'm free, but I'm travelling
on the 11th – I don't have the flight info yet.
I might have to be at Heathrow at 6am
so I can't have a late one. Can you do
lunchtime instead?

Bored yet? This back-and-forth could go on for days or even weeks, until eventually one person completely forgets to reply – in which case the whole palaver plays out all over again a month later. Or maybe the stars align and we meet for dinner, only for one of us to inevitably have to rush off to the next thing in the diary. It's ridiculous! If you're reading this and you can relate, then it should be a red flag. Trust me, busyness is overrated. I now accept that if I'm too busy for the things and the people that matter the most to me, then it is due to bad prioritisation, and I need to take a moment to reassess and reorder a few things.

This is why I now make sure I have what I call 'white space' in both my weekly schedule and my yearly calendar. I've named it 'white space' because it is exactly that: space on my calendar that has to remain white, and nothing can be added in. It is non-negotiable and I don't allow myself to fill it with anything. It's not a buffer of time to catch up on emails, or a free couple of hours to prepare for a podcast interview or to brainstorm ideas: it's white space to do, well, nothing. I have at least three hours of white space in my schedule each week, usually on a Thursday afternoon. Some people might say that it's contradictory for me to get up at 5:30am every day only to spend three hours on a Thursday doing nothing, but I want to take a hammer to this idea that getting up early is just about being productive and doing *more*. Admittedly, it started out that way for me, but over the last few years I've found that by getting up early and starting my day on my own terms, it actually allows me to have the time and energy to enjoy things like white space later on in the day.

Initially, the idea of simply doing nothing for a few hours felt very counterintuitive. Italians have a phrase, *dolce far niente,* which means 'the sweetness of doing nothing'. The concept is to *enjoy* doing nothing. It comes as no surprise to me that we don't have an equivalent in the English language. We associate idleness with laziness and unproductivity. The idea that you could choose to do nothing and *enjoy it* is literally a foreign concept. It's easy to go from one thing to the next, all day every day – working, working out, responding to emails, driving, shopping, reading, more emails, then eat, sleep, repeat. If every hour of every day is accounted for, then we miss out on life's random chances. We don't allow time for spontaneous fun, last-minute invitations, opportunities to play and learn, and time to just pause and take in the view. Plus, it's much harder to be creative and think of something original when we are constantly taking in information, ideas and noise from others.

White space takes some time to get used to if, like me, your default mode is 'doing'. You might find it uncomfortable to simply do nothing. So I try to avoid the temptation to listen to a podcast or even read a book, and instead embrace the silence of solitude. A simple way to start is to go out for a long walk and leave your phone at home. If you don't enjoy seated meditation, walking meditation can be a good alternative, but remember the point is to do nothing, so don't overthink or even plan it.

*

What about money, the reality that 'I can't afford to pursue my passion'?

This is something that comes up a lot, and it's understandably a concern for many people. Let's be real – whether you're a young single person living in an expensive city like London, or you're a parent with a mortgage and childcare costs, we all have financial commitments that we need to take care of. Don't worry, I'm not going to suggest that you quit your job and sell all of your belongings to fund your passion project. While you could argue that this *is* a viable option, it's unlikely that many of us would actually follow that advice. I like to think in a more practical way, and I think there are three clear options you have if you find that money is the obstacle stopping you from pursuing your passion.

Option A: Find a way to fund your passion project, or even better to make money from it alongside your current job. Once you're confident that you can sustain a consistent income from your side hustle, then you could consider reducing your hours at your current job to part-time, or going freelance. I spoke to happiness consultant Samantha Clarke on the importance of creating a 'financial runway'. 'I never advise people to quit, because as soon as you're focused on *how will I pay the bills?*, you'll end up making very narrow choices,' she suggested. 'Instead you need to create a runway, so if you want to leave your job in six months

/ nine months / twelve months, what's the runway that you'll need? How much do you need to save in order to be able to do this? You have to sit down and be really practical. Ask yourself how much you value security. How well do you cope with risk-taking and uncertainty? These are all important things to consider before you decide to leave your job.'

Could you dedicate your Power Hour each morning for the next six months to creating a side hustle or passion project? It's just one hour a day, but think of each one as laying another brick in the path that's taking you closer to your goal. Samantha agrees that the Power Hour is a great place to start. 'It might be that you have to carve out more time by getting up earlier to do what's necessary,' she concurred. 'Treat it as an experiment, then in a few months reflect back and assess the results. We've all got the same number of hours in a day; it's up to us how we choose to use them.'

Option B: Create a business that aligns with your purpose, so that it becomes an income stream. I would advise seeking financial advice from a business coach or financial advisor who can give you guidance and insight about how to gain investment and funding.

After working with fitness technology start-up Fiit for the last three years, I've witnessed what it really takes to create and sustain a business in the start-up world. The reality is that in order to run a business and employ a team, purpose-led or not, you still have to make a profit. The good news is that you can do both: purpose and profit are not mutually exclusive. Author and motivational speaker Simon Sinek's TED talk, 'How great leaders inspire action' (based on his bestselling book *Start With Why*), has been viewed by more than 50 million people and has been translated into 48 languages. Sinek created a powerful yet simple model for leadership, to help businesses and brands find their 'why'. Essentially, his framework encourages businesses to lead with purpose. The idea is that doing so will give you the confidence you need to make decisions, because there is no ulterior motive or conflict of interest. Leading with purpose will help you to hire people that share similar values, and it allows you to be clear about the company's objectives. Similarly, global entrepreneur and author Arianna Huffington believes that 'one of the most important skills for a CEO – and one that is only going to increase in importance – is finding and maintaining a sense of purpose.' She explains: 'Many people think of purpose as something that's fixed, but purpose is actually a skill, one that can be built and nurtured throughout an organization so that everyone within the company has internalized what the company stands for beyond profits and growth.' Creating a purpose-led business won't guarantee success, but it will make each (inevitable) mistake worthwhile, and knowing that you're creating something meaningful can be the fuel you need to get up out of bed and go to work everyday.

Option C: Simply enjoy your passion without making it your work or attaching any financial reward to it. Sounds crazy, right? Maybe your passion could be a fun hobby – remember those? Once upon a time, pre-internet, people had hobbies just for the sake of enjoyment. Imagine not having the pressure to monetise everything. Today, there is a common narrative that if you're good at something or have a creative skill, then you should sell it. If you're good at baking, you should sell your cakes. If you're good at yoga, then why not pack your bags and head off to India to become a yoga teacher? The notion that we can enjoy our hobbies and allow them to remain just that might feel radical, but it really shouldn't. If your passion brings you joy and fulfilment, then pursuing it might not have anything to do with earning money at all. As soon as you start to get paid for something, the transaction changes your intention. Maybe for you, using your morning Power Hour to create a life that you love means waking up at 5am to go surfing in the sea. You're never going to quit your job to go pro, but you're still waking up to doing what you love, every single day. Now *that's* time well spent.

*

The last thing that holds most people back from pursuing their passions and purpose is fear. Fear is an essential emotion: we cannot, nor should we want to, eliminate it. We develop fears about things we believe to be harmful, painful or dangerous to us. Many of our fears are rational: a good example is a fear of heights and falling. It might seem obvious, but we understand that if we fall from something very tall, there is a high probability that we will get hurt, and our brain brings that risk to our attention at the right time in order to keep us safe. We also have irrational fears (phobias), which is when we experience a fear response to something that is unlikely to cause us any harm, such as spiders or birds. The body's fear response is often called 'fight or flight', and it can either propel you forwards by forcing you to take action (fight), or send you running in the opposite direction (flight). Both reactions are designed to keep you safe. But there is a third way that we can respond to fear, and that is to do absolutely nothing. Fear can momentarily paralyse you, essentially keeping you stuck. This is the reaction I believe stops most people from making changes or taking risks.

I have interviewed business coach and author Jody Shield twice on the Power Hour podcast. Jody is an incredible woman who knows all about leading with purpose. In her twenties, she was working for an ad agency in London, and from the outside, her life seemed fun, glamorous and fast-paced. For Jody, the reality was very different. Back then, she was 'addicted to busy', exhausted and at the edge of burnout. As a result, Jody became ill and felt as though she'd reached her breaking point. So, she decided to impulsively book a one-way ticket to South America in search of something new. The rest is history, as they say. (If you want to hear the full story you can listen to her interview on the podcast. Just search: 'Power Hour, Jody Shield, November 2018'.) That one powerful decision changed the trajectory of Jody's entire life, and since then she has helped thousands of individuals and business owners to discover their purpose and live life on their own terms.

As she is someone who literally woke up one day and decided to travel to the other side of the world, you might assume that Jody is simply unafraid to take risks or make changes, but that's not the case. We all feel fear, but we don't have to respond to it in the same way. I asked Jody how she would describe her ideas around fear and what techniques she uses to manage anxiety, nervousness and self-doubt. She explained that she often experiments with cold water therapy, and how facing fear in a controlled environment can be incredibly beneficial.

When we step into an ice-cold shower or we get into an ice bath, we start to expand our belief of what's possible. So, when you think about having a cold shower, immediately your mindset shifts and you go into some sort of fight-or-flight response. You start to think, *Oh my gosh, cold water is awful, I don't want to step into it.* For me, I've always been someone who wants to expand; I want to outgrow my own limiting beliefs and fears and so cold water therapy was a really great test ground. It was a stimulator to walk into something that my mind would deem as threatening, and to start to understand what it was that my mind was telling me in those moments . . . I used to hate cold showers, so as I walked into the cold water, I would witness my mind's reaction trying to get me out of it. Literally, it would do whatever it could, shouting at me, 'Jody, this is dangerous, you need to get out.' . . . I decided that I was just going to breathe through it and allow myself to really feel the entire experience, because I know that every time I do this and resist the impulse to run away, I am expanding and growing. That is why cold water therapy can be good at helping people who suffer from anxiety and trauma, because often these emotions are masked behind our fear.

I've also heard this sort of experiment described as 'fear rehearsing': the idea is that if you rehearse how you will respond to fear in a situation you have control over, then the next time that inevitable fear-inducing moment arrives, you'll be better able to cope and manage your response. This technique is often used by free solo rock-climbers before they attempt to ascend massive (and potentially deadly) rock faces. Being able to remain calm becomes a matter of life and death when climbing: one wrong move as a result of panicking could literally be the last thing they ever do. Yikes!

In a (somewhat less intense) situation such as going to a job interview or a first date, fear and self-confidence are often two sides of the same coin. When I first started the podcast, I realised I was very comfortable talking about topics I knew a lot about – such as health, fitness and entrepreneurship – but as soon as I found myself at the edge of my understanding about a certain topic, my confidence would plummet and I would hold back on commenting or offering an opinion because I was afraid to say the wrong thing. In order to become a better interviewer, and to get over the fear of making a mistake, I decided to do two things. Firstly, and most simply, I knew that I needed to prepare and learn as much as possible about the guest before sitting down to interview them. I created a process for coming up with my talking points and questions for each episode, and it starts with scrolling through their social media to see what they are currently talking about. Then I visit their website and search online for any other interviews that they have done. If they've written a book, I'll read it; if they've done a TED talk, I'll watch it. As you can imagine, this is very time-consuming – especially when you consider that I release a new episode every week – but that is how I am able to ask the right questions and understand where my guests' answers are coming from. They always seem to appreciate the in-depth preparation – either that or they think I am a super fan! But I think that the intense prep work pays off. So next time you're feeling fearful or nervous about an upcoming event or situation, do as much preparation as you can and find a way to 'fear rehearse'. You'll walk in feeling way more confident knowing that, at the very least, you've put adequate time and effort in.

The second thing I did was accept that the only way to get better at hosting the podcast was through exposure. I learned each week through practice and repetition. Some guests would give me very short answers to my opening question, and I'd have to think fast and work really hard to draw out a more in-depth response. Other guests might talk for ten minutes without stopping, and I'd have to resist the urge to interrupt or add commentary. I'd listen back to the recording and try to identify annoying verbalisms and phrases that I could hear myself repeating too often. Over time, these processes helped me to build my confidence as a podcast host. No one starts out as a pro, and the paradox of progress means that the more we learn, the less we know. So don't be afraid to make mistakes. Accept that neither you nor your work will ever be perfect, and just do it anyway!

Please don't let fear be the thing that stops you from pursuing your passions. Do you know what is even more scary than failure? Inaction. If you try and fail, you'll survive, but if you never even dare to take that step, then you'll never know what you could have achieved. Inaction is the biggest risk of all.

*

We've established that life is short, the hourglass is filling up and we're running out of summers. (I'm breathing into a brown paper bag here.) But as much as I live my life with a sense of urgency and I think you should too, that doesn't mean that we need to panic or rush. This chapter is not intended to make you drop everything and start over; it's here to help you zoom out and look at the whole picture. To step out of your day-to-day routine and question what you *really* want to get out of each day. Being aware of time doesn't mean that we are racing to beat it. The day you plant the seed is not the day you eat the fruit, and often that time in between requires patience.

Patience is not a virtue that was given to me. I'm naturally a very impatient person, but the one thing that changed this for me was motherhood. I have an unlimited amount of patience for children – unfortunately, I haven't yet figured out how to extend that same grace to adults. (They should know better!) Last year, I sat down to interview legendary broadcaster and DJ Trevor Nelson, and I really agree with his view on patience.

Whenever the younger generation – anyone who wants to get into music or broadcasting – stops me and asks for advice, I'll give a minute and some advice, but I don't have all the answers. It's really important people try to work out how to carve their own path. My path was like digging a tunnel with a pickaxe, chipping away, chipping away, and before you know it, ten years have passed and you're still going, still chipping. You don't know where the other end of the tunnel is, and there's no one ahead of you to follow, but you just keep on going, chipping away. But the younger generation today, the problem is they can see right through the tunnel, they can see the other end and they want to get there as quickly as possible. It's a big problem because everything is so quick and accessible today. You have to have work ethic and to stay hungry.

The way I see it is: it doesn't matter how long it takes you to chip away in that tunnel, as long as you're going in the right direction. Hard work is never wasted, especially when you're doing something of meaning and value.

I've spent a lot of time thinking about my purpose. My focus and where I place emphasis in my life has changed considerably over the last ten years, but today I have a laser-focused purpose. In fact, I have built my life and career around it – and ultimately, it is what led me to starting the Power Hour podcast and to writing this book. Put simply, my purpose is to prove that ordinary people can achieve extraordinary things: I believe that we are all capable of *so* much more, and I try to lead by example. I'm not a professional athlete, I'm not a celebrity, I'm not exceptionally talented at any one thing – *but* I am hard-working, audacious and willing to learn. (An understatement: I'm obsessed with learning.) I've identified my own strengths and weaknesses and I'm willing to try and sometimes fail. In order to tell people how or what to do, I must attempt to show them. I believe this is what has enabled me to get to where I am today.

We are all here on this planet for an undetermined number of years – some people will have more than others – and those years can be condensed into a handful of important moments. Everything else will quickly be forgotten. If you live to be 80 years old and you look back on your life, what will those important, truly memorable moments be for you? What will you be known and remembered for? Raising a family? Building a business? Travelling the world? Writing books? Fighting for justice? Making people laugh? Those important moments are the things that will ultimately give your life meaning – and *purpose*.

Reward
yourself
for your
effort and
willingness
to try,
regardless
of the
outcome.

Create Your Own Power Hour

There have been many books written about morning routines, rituals and the daily habits of highly effective people – and I've read most of them. One thing they all agree on is that the very first hour of your day is critical. It impacts your energy, mood and decision-making for the rest of the day, so I've become very intentional about how I use that time. For the past four years I've started my day with an early-morning Power Hour, and over that time, I've learned how to get the best out of one hour. I've figured out which things to include, and which to avoid. I've experimented with different routines, using the Power Hour to focus on optimising one area of my life at a time: for a few months it's all about movement and training, then it shifts and becomes all about reading and learning, then journaling and prayer. For a while, it was dedicated solely to writing this book. My Power

Hour is constantly changing and evolving, but the daily practice remains consistent.

Take the tools, ideas and advice in this book to create a Power Hour of your own. Start with *why*, then consider *what* you need to do and *how* you're going to do it. Experimentation requires trial and error, so don't expect a 100 per cent success rate straight away. You might have a few false starts; you might get distracted or derailed by something unexpected. I get it, life happens. My suggestion in that case is don't dwell on it and don't use it as an excuse. Hit reset and try again. Go back a few chapters in this book and look for something you've underlined – find that page, story or quote that resonated with you and reread it. If my Power Hour doesn't work for you, try someone else's. The key is to keep adapting and refining it until you discover the ideal routine for *you*.

At the start of this book, I shared my ideas about developing a growth mindset and taking ownership of your decisions, and my belief that you should not allow your past circumstances to dictate your future. When I interview people on the Power Hour podcast,

I'll often start off by asking them to talk about their own personal story: where they grew up, what they liked at school, how they got started in their industry, and so on. What's most interesting to me about this introduction is that, by hearing the guest tell their own story, it gives us a clear understanding of their perception of it. The *way* they talk about their story showcases their beliefs and their mindset. How they view their setbacks and failures, opportunities and achievements, and the way they talk about other people in their story (such as their parents, friends and colleagues) – all of it is a window into how they view the world.

For example, if someone tells me, 'I had to try really hard at school – I wasn't the smartest kid in the class and I struggled to keep up. I never went to university, so I started working sooner and gained a lot of experience, which gave me a head start in my career,' I immediately think: this person has a growth mindset. They view a perceived disadvantage, such as not going to university, as an advantage.

They could have said, 'School was difficult for me, I'm not smart enough, so I never had the chance to go to university. I've worked harder than everyone else to get to where I am today.' You could argue that both versions are true, but the important question is: which version do you tell yourself?

What's your story? What is that story costing you? Everyone is unique: our experiences shape our perception of the world and how we view ourselves within it. So, are you taking ownership and responsibility for where you are today? Do you believe that you have the ability to create your future, yourself and your life? Have you always told your story as though you are a victim of bad luck and unfortunate circumstances? How can you start to tell yourself a more empowering story – a story in which you have the desire and the ability to pursue your goals and live up to your fullest potential? Not *because* of your past but *in spite* of it.

Ultimately, all that matters is the story *you* believe to be true.

Imagine this: exactly one year from today, you're sitting outside a cafe drinking coffee with a friend, and you're telling them that you've just had the best year of your life. What would need to happen in the next 365 days to make *that* story true? Start with your end goal in mind, and then reverse through the steps that you'll need to take to get there. Maybe you need to change your job or start working out. Perhaps you need to meet some new people, or you need to learn a new skill, or start saving some money. Whatever it is that you need to start doing to make that happen, start doing it *today*. Yes, the best time to plant a tree was 20 years ago – but the second-best time is right now. You can never go back in time; you can only move forwards from this very moment. Don't allow a fixed mindset or your negative beliefs to keep you stuck in the same story. Start using your Power Hour to work on a new one.

I've written this entire book throughout 2020 – a year that will leave the world forever changed. As a result of working in isolation during this strange and uncertain time, loomed over by a global pandemic, I've learned to value the small things and take joy in the everyday. At the same time, I'm constantly looking ahead to the future and believing that the best is yet to come. Although 2020 wasn't the year I had planned, and it certainly wasn't the year I got everything I wanted, for me, 2020 was the year I learned to treasure impermanence and truly value time. More than ever before, I now understand the fragility of life. Nothing is permanent, nothing will last forever. The beautiful thing about impermanence is that it makes you appreciate everything more, because you recognise that one day it will be gone. And at the same time, it diminishes the importance of life's day-to-day stresses, because in a small number of weeks, months or years, today's biggest problem will no longer mean anything to you. It won't matter. As a mother, I am acutely aware of time passing. With each day, I watch my son outgrow his clothes. The little boy who used to fall asleep on my shoulder as I carried him will soon be taller than me.

As I said before, time is the most valuable thing we have, and it is the one thing that we can never get back once it's gone, so we have to make it count. The Power Hour is more important today than it's ever been before.

*

How much do you *value* your time? People often invest a lot more energy and thought into managing their finances than they do into managing their time. You can make money, spend money, win money, lose money, and you can ask for a refund to get wasted money back – but the same cannot be said about time.

When you look at your calendar, what do you see? Is it blank? If there is a lot of empty space, maybe this is because you don't feel the need to plan your time and you prefer to just go with the flow. The problem with that is that there will always be demands for your time by something or someone, and if you're not intentional about how you use it, it can be very easy to give all of your time away. Or maybe your calendar is absolutely full of neatly colour-coded blocks, and every hour of every day is marked out. This is why we all need a morning Power Hour: so we can get focused and reclaim our time. I use the word 'reclaim' intentionally when telling people about the Power Hour, because when you *reclaim* something, you are taking back what was previously yours, which was lost or stolen.

What's something that you want to do this week that you usually *don't* have time for? Each week we all have

168 hours to spend, so let's break it down and see if we can reclaim just seven of them.

Let's say you work 9:00am to 6:00pm for five days each week; that's a total of 45 hours.

If you sleep for an average of eight hours each night, that's a total of 56 hours.

$$45 + 56 = 101$$

Okay, we've still got 67 hours left. *Excuse me?* Yes, that's right: 67 hours remaining. Check it for yourself and you'll see that my calculations are correct. (This is why I've always liked maths – numbers don't lie.)

Deduct six more hours a week for commuting. Even if you were to spend one hour each evening watching TV, you'd still be left with 54 hours.

I think you get the point. The bottom line is that most of us are pretty bad at managing our time, and as a result we waste so much of it. I don't think it's realistic, nor is it useful, to schedule every hour of every day – we need some 'white space' – but let's at least take one hour, the first hour, each day to do something valuable.

If you think that taking an hour at the start of each day for yourself is in any way selfish or self-indulgent, then I'm here to tell you that I'm sorry, but you're wrong. We've all heard the flight attendant instructing us to put on our own oxygen mask before helping others, because we're better equipped to take care of those we love when we've taken care of ourselves. The same rule applies here too. We've been taught to believe that we must always put others before ourselves, and that consciously prioritising other people's needs is a noble and gracious thing to do. But consider this: if you were in hospital and you needed to have surgery, would you rather have a doctor who was well-rested and alert, or a doctor who was overly tired because they'd been selflessly working late for the third night in a row? I know which one I'd choose. The reality is that your health, relationships, kids and work will all benefit from you reclaiming some time and energy to invest in yourself. You cannot give what you don't have.

But how much difference can one hour really make? Well, if you're familiar with the theory of marginal gains, then you'll know that small things can have a very big impact. The theory explores how small, incremental improvements in any process can lead to a significant overall improvement when added together. The concept is often described as the '1 per cent rule', to highlight that even though 1 per cent might seem like a meaningless amount, it can, in fact, change everything. This innovative concept was made famous by the former performance director of British Cycling, Sir Dave Brailsford. His idea was to focus on cyclists' key stats, such as power output, and highlight areas of weakness in order to make improvements to the smallest of details – the 1 per cent. Initially, people mocked his approach, but they later witnessed the undeniable results. Under Brailsford's guidance, Team GB topped the cycling medal table at both the 2008 and 2012 Olympics, winning eight gold medals at each.

If a 1 per cent improvement can create such great results for some of the best athletes in the world, then I'm pretty sure that dedicating 4 per cent of your day (one hour) to any of your goals is going to be worth the effort. Sure, one hour might not be enough to revolutionise your entire life, but over time it certainly will be impactful. Doing something once or twice won't make much difference; you have to be consistent.

*

Your Power Hour is customisable, but the one non-negotiable is that it should be the *first* hour of your day. By making it the first thing you do when you wake up, you're emphasising its importance in your life and putting it at the top of your priority list, and it's also a great way to overcome procrastination. If you are an expert procrastinator, then you know everything there is to know about delaying important tasks until the very last moment. If procrastination is one of your non-useful habits, then the Power Hour just might be the perfect antidote. Typically, we put off doing things on our to-do list for one (or more) of the following reasons:

> ▸ We're attempting to do something that we are not very good at, so the task seems overwhelming and difficult. If you're not good at managing your personal finances, you might put off doing your tax return for as long as possible, for example. Just the

thought of doing it makes you shudder, so you delay it again and again. You know you'll get around to it eventually, right?

▶ We put off things that we said yes to a while ago and now we *really* wish that we hadn't. A few years ago, my business coach gave me some fantastic advice on this issue. She said, 'When someone asks you to do something and the deadline is in a few weeks' time, before you respond take a moment and ask yourself, *Would I say yes if I had to do this tomorrow?*' That one question was a game changer for me! If I'm not excited by the thought of doing it tomorrow, then the reality is I'm not going to be any more enthusiastic in two weeks' time either.

▶ We prioritise the things on our list that are the most fun and rewarding over the more boring (but often more important) tasks. We tell ourselves that we're not intentionally putting things off until the last minute, but that we've taken on too much and we're *just too busy* at the moment. This is simply avoidance in disguise.

So how could the Power Hour help you overcome all of these procrastination tactics? It's simple: pick a day, towards the start of the week, and use that day's Power Hour to 'swallow the frog'. And no, I don't mean literally swallow a frog. I'm talking about doing the one thing on your list that you *really* don't want to do – the thing you vowed to do last week but that is still incomplete. Underline this task (the metaphorical frog), and then use your Power Hour to get that *one* thing done first. Take it from someone who could teach university seminars in procrastination – the swallow-the-frog tactic is one which will save you a lot of wasted time and stress later on. If time is money, then procrastination is a credit card: you can spend as much as you like today, but you'll have to pay for it eventually. Starting your day by doing something you're dreading might not sound appealing, but once it's done, you'll feel a sense of relief and freedom.

At the very start of this book, I said that it doesn't really matter what time your Power Hour is, so long as it is the first hour of your day. Forgive me for unintentionally misleading you, but seven chapters later and I've changed my mind. (Remember, we've agreed we like change – change is good!) The time of day actually does matter. In order to get the most out of it, the Power Hour needs to be early – and this is why . . .

In short: before 6:00am, the rest of the world is asleep and you can focus without interruptions and distractions. If, like me, you are easily distracted, then you might find it difficult to concentrate on one single task unless you are in solitude. Scientist and author Cal Newport explains that we're quickly losing our capacity to concentrate for an extended period of time on a demanding task, but it's an incredibly valuable ability. He calls this meta-skill 'deep work'. If you practise doing deep work (which we can do, Newport says, if we 'ditch the tech' and 'embrace the boredom'), 'you'll become much better at what you do, and you'll achieve more in less time'. Basically, when we try to do two or more things at once, we may *think* that we are saving time, but it's actually *less* effective. The stats support his ideas too. Countless studies have shown that attempting to multitask reduces our cognitive function and productivity by up to 40 per cent. Each time we shift from one task to another, it takes our brain time to refocus. How many times have you sat in front of your laptop to do one thing, while looking up every few minutes to speak to someone, all while having your phone at the ready to quickly reply to inbound messages and notifications? It's no wonder we can't get any work done!

The honest truth is that, at 5:30am, I do not feel the constant temptation to look at my phone, check emails, scroll through social media or chat to anyone. I allow myself to focus and achieve deep work much more easily. Nobody is expecting you to even be awake, let alone be online or available. This is one of the things I enjoy most about the Power Hour, and that environment is harder to cultivate later in the day. If you're studying or working on something that requires a lot of concentration, try doing it first thing in the morning as part of your Power Hour. Make sure your phone is out of sight, and close all other web browsers and tabs on your computer. You'll be amazed at how much you can achieve in just that one hour without distractions. When I work in this way, I always start my day feeling noticeably calmer. If I send out emails that require action first thing, I am being *pro*active rather than *re*active, and I can move on to the next task without that nagging feeling that someone is waiting for me to get back to them. I also feel happier because I know that, as a result of that one hour of deep work before dawn, I've probably just saved myself two hours of time doing less effective work later on in the day.

The idea that the Power Hour must be early (ideally before 6:00am) is partly due to the scheduling and organisation of the rest of the world. Whether you're heading out to work, dropping off kids at school or starting to work from home, the world typically gets going between 8:00am and 9:00am. If you're still lying in bed at 7:00am, then you're not going to have much time to spare. This explains why I've witnessed so many people getting ready for work while on public transport: applying their make-up while standing up on the

Underground (mastering eyeliner is tricky at the best of times, so I'm equal parts impressed and confused at how it is even possible to do this on a moving vehicle) or eating their breakfast on the train. (And I'm not just talking about a standard Pret coffee and croissant combo. I've seen people eating granola out of Tupperware, and I once watched a guy slicing a whole pineapple during rush hour on the Jubilee line. True story.) Perhaps the most socially unacceptable behaviour I've seen while commuting in London was a man using nail clippers to trim his fingernails. Gross! Some things absolutely must happen *before* you leave the house.

Most people will claim that they hate being late and yet they allow themselves very little time to get ready in the morning. (One friend in particular springs to mind. She is *always* late.) Never mind meditating, working out and sending emails: if you go from your bed to your desk in less than an hour, it's not going to set you up for a good day. Personally, I know that if I'm running late or rushing around in the morning, I feel frantic and kind of anxious. Occasionally, this can't be avoided (especially when children are involved – they have no concept of time; no matter how many times you tell them when they need to be ready to leave the house, rest assured they'll still be doing things at the last minute), but the easiest and most obvious solution? That's right, you guessed it, I'm still beating that drum: *get up earlier.*

More time = less stress.

*

So, you're getting up early each day and you've decided what it is you're going to work towards, but how do you turn what feels like a faraway goal into something real and achievable? I have five rules when it comes to goal-setting, and I follow them in this order:

1. Get specific

2. Set a deadline

3. Tell someone

4. Assess and reflect

5. Ask for help

1. Get specific.

This is the first rule, and for good reason. By definition, the word 'focus' means directing your attention and effort. If you do not start out with a clear goal, then you'll be unsure of where to direct your focus. This is advice that has been around since the beginning of time: even the Bible tells us to be definitive about our requests – 'Write the vision, make it clear'. Having a vague goal such as 'I want to start a business' or 'I want to get fit' isn't going to be enough to get you out of bed at 6:00am every day. Getting a spark of inspiration or a new idea is a great place to start, but you then need to go deeper to figure out exactly what you want and *why* you want it. The first step is to ask yourself these four questions:

Why do you want to do this?

Who will benefit from this?

How are you going to achieve it?

What could get in the way or stop you from making it happen?

If you're still not getting to the heart of your goal, and are struggling to answer that first question in a meaningful way, try this simple exercise:

Ask 'Why?' five times

Goal: I want to write a book.

Why do you want to write a book?
Because books are a great way to reach more people.

Why do you want to reach more people?
To share my ideas and the concept of the Power Hour.

Why do you want to share the idea of the Power Hour?
The Power Hour has revolutionised my life, and by sharing it I can encourage others to pursue their goals and create a life they love.

Why do you want to encourage people to create a
life they love?
Because I believe that most people will never
even come close to reaching their full potential,
just because their goals are too small and they
limit themselves.

Why do you believe this?
Because I used to do this too, and deep down
I have a fear of looking back on my life with
regrets. I *never* want to say, 'I always wanted
to do X but didn't get the chance.'

When you ask yourself 'Why?' five times, you'll get
to the bottom of what your goal is really all about. I'd
never written a book before, but I knew from the very
start that it was not going to be an easy thing to do,
and having a vague goal might not have been enough
to keep me energised and focused throughout the
process. So at 5:30am on a Saturday morning, when
I'd sit at my kitchen table, open my laptop and start to
write, I had those questions and answers in my mind. I

had to imagine that, one day, someone could read this thing I'd written and that it would resonate with them – just like that middle key on the piano. If even just one person reads this book and it encourages them to take action and to make meaningful changes to their life, then I will have achieved my goal.

Hopefully you now have a very specific goal. You know why, who, how and what it's going to take. The next thing that you need to do is . . .

2. Set a deadline.

This is absolutely critical! It's hard to stand at a start line without knowing if or when there will be a finish line. Personally, I *have* to have a deadline to work towards. Not only does it keep me motivated, but more importantly it helps me to prioritise my time. If I've got three weeks to go until my next race, I won't skip training. I will reschedule things in my diary if necessary, to make sure that I don't miss any sessions. But without that pending goal, I'm much more likely to skip a training run because it feels less important if there is no real consequence.

Typically, we will stretch out a project to use as much time as we are given, even if it can be done more quickly. So whatever your goal is, set yourself a deadline, and be as specific as possible. Six months? Too vague. I want you to pick a date and circle it on your calendar. Having a time pressure will force you to prioritise your goal, so work out exactly how many months, weeks and days you have, and then get to work. If you know you're the kind of person that leaves things until the last minute, then set yourself a fake deadline that is one week earlier than the real one. Shift everything accordingly, and literally force yourself to believe that this new deadline is fixed. That way, if you meet the deadline, you can either take a well-deserved break or have an extra week to refine and perfect it. And if you don't make the fake deadline, you've got an extra week's grace to keep going.

3. Tell someone.

(I'd like to caveat this next part by saying: consider *who* that somebody is. Make sure you're telling somebody who wants to see you succeed.)

Here's why I think it's important that you tell someone else about your goals. The most obvious reason is accountability: when you tell your friend about your new business idea, it not only forces you to refine the idea before you share it with them, but you'll also feel like you'll need to have made progress by the next time you see them, because they'll inevitably ask you for an update. Some people like the feeling of accountability as it accelerates their progress, and for others the pressure can be overwhelming. Only you know whether this is going to help you move closer to your goals. For me, the more people I tell, the better! In fact, if I have an idea and I haven't told anyone about it within a week, that is usually a red flag and it tells me that I'm not really that excited about it and should probably focus my time and energy elsewhere.

Make sure you communicate to the other person why you are telling them about your goal. Are you asking for their opinion? Will you be upset or offended if they think it's a bad idea? Are you telling them because you just need someone to be a sounding board, but you've already made up your mind that you're going to do it? Have you chosen to tell this person because they have experience in this area and so might be able to support and guide you? Set out your expectations at the start to avoid feeling disheartened or derailed if you don't get the response that you want. That's why I started off by saying to consider *who* that someone is: which member of your board of directors is the best one to talk to about this particular goal?

4. Assess and reflect.

You've outlined a specific goal, set a deadline, shared it with a friend and been working hard for six weeks. It's now time to pause, assess where you're at, and reflect on what's working so far and what maybe isn't going so well. Whether the end result of this goal is to improve your health, make more money or progress at work, you have to be able to measure your success in a way that is real and quantifiable. Outline some progress markers that you can look at objectively in order to make sure you're moving in the right direction. How are you measuring your progress? What information do you need to know in order to make adjustments and improvements? Avoid the temptation to move so fast and so far that you fail to notice when you're veering off the track. It's like if you're steering a ship and you're heading off course by even ten degrees – the sooner you can correct it, the better.

This is also a great time to ask for feedback and to self-evaluate. According to psychologist and researcher Dr Tasha Eurich, 95 per cent of people think they are self-aware, but in fact, only about 10 per cent *actually* are. That's pretty shocking. Fortunately, she also says that: 'One thing that is abundantly clear from all of the empirical research on the topic of self-awareness is that becoming more self-aware is something that we can all learn to do.' She defines self-awareness as the will and the skill to see ourselves more clearly. It can be categorised in two ways: internal self-awareness and external self-awareness. Internal self-awareness is when we understand ourselves from the inside out; it's knowing who we are, what our values are, and understanding our unique strengths and weaknesses. Equally important is external self-awareness. This is self-awareness from the outside in: the ability to understand how other people see us. I was surprised to learn that they are completely independent from each other. While your internal self-awareness may be accurate, your external self-awareness could be way off, and vice versa. If you're caught out or surprised by other people's comments (e.g. 'You're always *so* competitive'), this could indicate a lack of external self-awareness.

Dr Eurich's research concludes that people who score highly on the self-awareness scale are better communicators, better leaders and better parents, and are less likely to lie, cheat and steal. They're happier and have deeper, more trusting relationships. Sounds pretty good to me! One of the ways in which we can all improve our own self-awareness is to get feedback from a variety of different people. That might sound pretty daunting, but keep an open mind and remember that your reason for doing this is to improve and to move you closer to your goals. Ask people for both positive and negative feedback in order to get a full picture. When people ask for feedback, they often assume that they only need to identify weaknesses in order to improve, but it's just as valuable to understand your strengths.

5. Ask for help.

Not because you feel as though you *need* help, but because, if nothing else, asking for help will undoubtedly speed up the process of achieving your goal. In any given situation, the person who will learn the most is the person who is willing to ask the most questions. A common trap is that the more accomplished we become at something, the less likely we are to ask for support. We might think that we already know enough about the topic or project to go it alone, or we might worry that, by asking for help, we are highlighting gaps in our knowledge. My view is that if someone is willing to ask for help, it means they care about getting it right. It can also be pretty humbling to admit that you don't have all the answers, and remembering this will help take the pressure off somewhat.

When it comes to asking others for help, I follow a simple approach. First, make sure you're asking the right person (meaning they have the skills or knowledge that you're missing). Second, make sure you're asking them at the right time. If your partner comes home late on a Friday night after an afternoon of intense meetings, it's probably not the best time to ask them to look over your keynote speech. Be considerate of the other person's frame of mind, and choose a moment when they're going to be willing and able to help you. Finally, ask without conditions or expectations. This one can be difficult, but it's really important. When you ask someone to help you, remember that it is a *request* and not an instruction. They are not obliged to say yes, so don't take it personally or feel angry if they say no. Maybe they don't feel as though they have time to fully commit to helping you, or maybe they just don't want to help – either way, let it go and do not keep a score chart. And never be disingenuous about why you are asking for help. I once had someone ask me to take part in a half-marathon in Portugal in order to raise money and awareness for a charity. I later found out that, before I'd even agreed to take part, they had used my name and photograph to promote the event and to convince some of my friends to join too. Honestly, I wouldn't have minded if they had just been upfront and sincere from the start, but this definitely made me hesitant to work with them.

I try to stress-test each of my goals against these five rules. So far, this framework has helped me to achieve more in less time – and it's also helped me to remain focused when shiny new distractions come along to tempt me down the rabbit hole. A really important thing to remember, however, is that although I've talked a lot throughout this book about defining your goals, it's even more important to make sure those goals do not define *you*. Ultimately, what really matters? Success can be defined in many different ways, and I don't want to succeed at the wrong things. I only want to succeed at the things that are important to *me*, things that align with my values and will impact the way I fundamentally feel about myself. You are not defined by whether or not you achieve every goal on your list today, this week or this year. Separate yourself from your goals and reward yourself for your effort and willingness to *try*, regardless of the outcome.

*

I've asked so many people about their morning routine, and by now you might be wondering how I spend my own Power Hour. Each day, my alarm is set for 5:30am (though I usually wake up roughly ten minutes before my alarm). I get up and head straight to the bathroom, rinse my face with cold water and take 10 to 12 deep and fast nasal breaths (inhaling through the nose/exhaling through the nose). During this breathing exercise, I try to focus on one word or short phrase, something that is meaningful to me and relevant to the day ahead. It can be as simple as 'see the good', so that no matter what happens that day or which direction it takes, no matter who I interact with, I will still try to see the good. Focusing on the good things, even if it's just for a minute or two, shifts my mindset for the rest of the day. Alternatively, if I'm focused on just one word, then it needs to be something powerful and simple, like 'courage'. I remind myself that it takes courage to go after big goals, it takes courage to put your ideas out there, it takes courage to do hard things.

All of this takes less than three minutes, so then I head downstairs and begin one of the following:

> ▶ A full 60 minutes dedicated to doing just one thing. This could be running, reading, admin or even cooking, but whatever it is,

I give myself the whole hour to focus on that one thing. This is how the Power Hour started for me, and it's simple and effective. Running is usually my go-to, especially in the spring and summer, because it ticks so many boxes. I listen to a podcast or an audiobook as I run (last year I listened to 49 books while running), so I'm getting my daily movement at the same time as learning something inspiring. Running in the morning never fails to make the rest of my day better.

▸ Two 30-minute sections: 30 minutes for my body and 30 minutes for my mind. I'll start off by rolling out a yoga mat, playing some energising music and then I move, stretch and breathe to wake up my body. I'll do a variety of exercises that get my heart rate up, but it's not too intense. Initially, I move slowly and do whatever I feel like doing, before transitioning into some of my favourite Pilates exercises to activate my core. This reminds me that I am in control, strong and can endure. Next, I'll do some full-body stretches, followed by a sequence of squats, lunges, planks and push-ups. I couldn't tell you how many I do, it's different every time. My rule is generally to do the exercise until you feel the burn – then do ten more. Finally, I finish off with some more stretching. (As a side note, I've become obsessed with Pilates lately. I cannot recommend it enough – I honestly think that if you only do one form of movement, it should be Pilates. It will tone and sculpt your body, protect your back and improve your posture, as well as making you a faster and more efficient runner. I really hope that I'll still be doing Pilates when I'm 80!) After 30 minutes of movement, my body feels energised, I'm wide awake and, crucially, my mind is switched on. I'll grab a pen and do 30 minutes of journaling, where I might write down the answers to my six questions (see page 42), or turn to a blank page and write down anything that comes to me. Sometimes, I write out a list of the following statements, to make sure my day heads towards my long-term and short-term goals: *This year I will . . . This month I will . . . This week I will . . . Today I will . . .* Disclaimer: I do have to keep one eye on the clock to make sure I don't run over the 30-minute window! I can very easily get carried away, and suddenly it's 7:00am.

▶ Three 20-minute blocks: 20 minutes of movement, 20 minutes of mindfulness and 20 minutes of *doing*. Personally, I don't do this one as often as the other options, but I know that it has been really effective for many people. The first 20 minutes of movement can be anything that gets your heart rate up and oxygen moving around the body. Power walking and jogging are both great for this. The second 20 minutes could be meditation or journaling, whatever gives you a moment of calm before your day starts. And the last 20 minutes are about action. Is there something on your to-do list that you could do in 20 minutes or less? Is there something you've been putting off which you could do to make the rest of the day a little bit better?

Whichever way you decide to spend your first hour, my advice is that you plan it and commit to it the day before (and not the night before, when you're tired).

Two things worth mentioning in relation to my Power Hour are my phone and my breakfast. Most days, I try to avoid using my phone before 6:30am – there's nothing that can't wait until after my Power Hour. I do take my phone with me when I'm running, to listen to a podcast and to use Strava (of course), but I avoid opening messages, emails or scrolling through social media. If I do open Instagram before 6:30am, then it is probably to share a message of encouragement and give a virtual high-five to those people who are also getting up and out before sunrise. As for breakfast, this doesn't happen for a few hours. Typically I'll eat breakfast at about 9:30am, when I get home from taking my son to school. This way I have enough time to prepare something and enjoy it without rushing.

*

Since I first started the Power Hour podcast in 2018, I've asked more than a hundred people about their Power Hour routines – from cold showers to making soup, surfing to boxing, morning raves to celery juice. I've interviewed pro footballers, bestselling authors, renowned doctors, psychologists, business coaches . . . the list goes on. I doubt I'll ever get bored of hearing people's stories and learning more about what motivates them to get out of bed in the morning. Now, it's over to you to create your own Power Hour: to focus on your goals and create a life you love.

The question that I ask each of my guests at the end of each episode is this: if you had one extra hour each day (yes, from now on there are going to be 25 hours in a day), what would you use that extra hour to do?

I've heard a lot of different answers to this question. Some guests tell me that they'd use the extra hour to read more books; others say they'd use the time to call their parents, practise the piano, meditate or write down their ideas for a new business plan. Whatever the specifics might be, it's typically the one thing that they'd love to do, if only they had *more* time.

I sincerely hope that reading this book has sparked ideas and given you some inspiration. I hope that you've learned something new, and I hope that, from now on, you will start your day with a Power Hour.

Finally, I'd like to ask you that same question.

If you had one extra hour each day, what would *you* use that hour to do?

Acknowledgements

I could not have written this book without the help, love and support of all of my people, past and present. Each of you has given me the confidence and the self belief to make this happen. My sister Ayeisha and my brother Alex, we've been together through it all. To Rob, thank you for every unforgettable milestone. My girls Hayley, AJ, Tash, Tara, Phoebe and Jules, your friendship means more to me than you know. My management team Jess, Flora, Louise and Ruby, you allow me to pursue my audacious goals. The Power Hour podcast team Jack, Winnie, Tom and Phie, thank you for believing in my idea and for making it a reality. The book team Micheline, Lydia, Najma and my editor Anna, our weekly Zoom call was a highlight of my lockdown week. Anna, working with you on this book has been an incredible experience. Thank you for your guidance, endless patience and words of encouragement. You helped me order my ideas and thoughts, and you helped me find my voice. I'm so grateful to everyone who read the early sample chapters and offered feedback along the way. Ben, Emma and Sammi, thank you for giving me your time and for allowing me to talk incessantly about *the book*. Special thank you to my adored son Jude, seeing the world through your eyes allows me to dream without limits.

Endnotes

The Power of Mindset

p. 19 'The terms "fixed mindset" . . .', Dr Carol S. Dweck, *Mindset: Changing the way you think to fulfil your potential* (London: Robinson, 2012).

p. 20 'It is not just . . .', Ibid.

p. 22 'In his book . . .', Thomas Suddendorf, *The Gap: The Science of What Separates Us from Other Animals* (New York: Basic Books, 2013).

p. 23 'the theatre of our minds', 'Seeing is believing . . .', Natalie Pennicotte-Collier, in conversation with me on the *Power Hour* podcast, 12 December 2019.

p. 26 'To an extent . . .', Lena Kessler, in conversation with me on the *Power Hour* podcast, 5 March 2019.

p. 28 'The key to success . . .', Stephen Covey, *The 7 Habits of Highly Effective People: Revised and Updated 30th Anniversary Edition* (New York: Simon & Schuster, 2020).

p. 28 'In his book *Outliers* . . .', Malcolm Gladwell, *Outliers: The Story of Success* (London: Penguin Books, 2008).

p. 33 'statistically I can expect . . .', 'Healing a divided Britain: the need for a comprehensive race equality strategy', report by the Equality and Human Rights Commission, published August 2016, available on www.equalityhumanrights.com.

p. 36 'It's good to know . . .', Maggie Alphonsi, in conversation with me on the *Power Hour* podcast, 22 October 2019.

p. 40 'One of the tools . . .', Jim Kwik, '138: Discovering Your Dominant Question' episode on the *Kwik Brain with Jim Kwik* podcast, 25 July 2019.

p. 43 'He explains that . . .', Ibid.

p. 47 'Plasticity exists from . . .', Norman Doidge, *The Brain That Changes Itself: Stories of Personal Triumph from the Frontiers of Brain Science* (London: Penguin Books, 2008).

p. 49 'In a world . . .', Lauren Armes, in conversation with me on the *Power Hour* podcast, 9 June 2020.

p. 52 'Gladwell's 10,000-Hour Rule', Gladwell, op. cit.

p. 54 'My two biggest lessons . . .', Brandon Stanton, in an interview with CNBC, December 2014, available on www.cnbc.com.

p. 56 'The ultimate endurance . . .', James Lawrence, 'How to Master Mental Toughness: James Lawrence on Impact Theory', interview on the *Impact Theory* podcast, 19 December 2017.

p. 58 'I made a decision . . .', Karl Lokko, in conversation with me on the *Power Hour* podcast, 22 January 2019.

How to Create Powerful Habits

p. 67 'In *The Power of Habit* . . .', Charles Duhigg, *The Power of Habit: Why We Do What We Do, and How to Change* (London: William Heinemann, 2012).

p. 68 'More recently, James Clear . . .', James Clear, *Atomic Habits: Tiny Changes, Remarkable Results* (London: Random House Business Books, 2018).

p. 70 'The ability to discipline . . .', Dr Maxwell Maltz, *Psycho-Cybernetics: Updated and Expanded* (New York: Perigree, 2015).

p. 74 'When I asked chartered . . .', Fiona Murden, in conversation with me on the *Power Hour* podcast, 3 January 2019.

p. 85 'revealed that most of us . . .', Tanya Goodin, as part of the panel for 'Daylesford Discusses: Wellness for a World that Never Switches Off' event, 24 February 2020.

The Power of Movement

p. 99 'You don't need...', Dr Rupy Aujla in conversation with me on the *Power Hour* podcast, 17 January 2019.

p. 99 'movement protects the...', Kimberley Wilson, *How to Build a Healthy Brain: Reduce stress, anxiety and depression and future-proof your brain* (London: Yellow Kite, 2020).

p. 107 'suggests that mirroring...', Jason G. Goldman, 'Why Dancing Leads to Bonding', *Scientific American*, 1 May 2016, available on www.scientificamerican.com.

p. 108 'Dance movement psychotherapy...', Kimberley Pena, in conversation with me on the *Power Hour* podcast, 31 May 2019.

p. 109 'The first hour...', Linzi Boyd, in conversation with me on the *Power Hour* podcast, 18 May 2020.

p. 110 'Life happens. Every...', Richie Norton, in conversation with me on the *Power Hour* podcast, 10 January 2019.

p. 119 'The average commute...', National Express Transport Solutions, 'Average London commute stands at 74 minutes a day', 25 September 2020, available on www.ne-transportsolutions.com.

p. 119 'A 2015 report...', 'Commuting and individual well-being in London', report by the Greater London Authority, January 2015, available on www.data.gov.uk.

p. 120 'Managing a busy . . .', Sammi Adhami, in conversation with me.

The Power of Sleep

p. 136 'In it, Walker explains . . .', 'routinely sleeping less . . .', 'Adults forty-five years . . .', Matthew Walker, *Why We Sleep: The New Science of Sleep and Dreams* (London: Allen Lane, 2017).

p. 137 'Sleep has been . . .', Jazmin Sawyers, in conversation with me on the *Power Hour* podcast, 8 January 2019.

p. 138 'Sleep underpins everything . . .', Dr Sophie Bostock, in conversation with me on the *Power Hour* podcast, 19 June 2019.

p. 140 'In the UK . . .', Marco Túlio de Mello et al., 'Sleep Disorders as a Cause of Motor Vehicle Collisions', *International Journal of Preventive Medicine*, 4(3): 246–257, 3 March 2013, available on www.ncwww.ncbi.nlm.nih.gov.

p. 144 'Sophie recommends keeping . . .', Dr Sophie Bostock, in conversation with me on the *Power Hour* podcast, 19 June 2019.

p. 146 'We are designed . . .', Ibid.

p. 148 'women will typically . . .', 'Gender pay gap in the UK: 2019', report by the Office for National Statistics, published October 2019, available on www.ons.gov.uk.

p. 148 'Throughout her lifetime . . .', Lizzie Thomson, 'Everything to know about the "gender sleep gap"', *Metro*, 17 August 2019.

p. 149 'It's down to our . . .', Dr Zoe Williams, in conversation with me on the *Power Hour* podcast, 4 June 2019.

p. 151 'You can change . . .', Ibid.

p. 154 'Shield artificial light . . .', National Sleep Foundation, 'How artificial light affects our sleep patterns', available on www.sleep.org.

p. 156 'Studies show that . . .', Alice Park, 'Why You Shouldn't Read a Tablet Before Bed', *Time Magazine*, 22 December 2014.

p. 158 'Scientifically, there may . . .', National Sleep Foundation, 'Food and Drink that Promote a Good Night Sleep', blog post available on www.uniquemindcare.com.

p. 158 'Dr Rangan Chatterjee suggests . . .', Dr Rangan Chatterjee, *The 4 Pillar Plan: How to Relax, Eat, Move and Sleep Your Way to a Longer, Healthier Life* (London: Penguin Life, 2017).

p. 160 'That is why . . .', Dr Sophie Bostock, in conversation with me on the *Power Hour* podcast, 19 June 2019.

p. 161 'This is why . . .', Ibid.

p. 165 'the power of the breath', Wim Hof, *The Wim Hof Method: Activate Your Potential, Transcend Your Limits* (London: Rider, 2020).

p. 165 'We are only . . .', James Nestor, '#1506 – James Nestor', interview on *The Joe Rogan Experience* podcast, 13 July 2020.

p. 166 'Health psychologist Kelly . . .', Kelly McGonigal, '374: Kelly McGonigal, The Upside of Stress', interview on *The Jordan Harbinger Show* podcast, 7 July 2020.

p. 167 'Kelly says that . . .', Ibid.

The Power of People

p. 171 'Alone, we can . . .', Helen Keller, in speech, available from the Helen Keller Archive at the American Foundation for the Blind (AFB).

p. 174 'What I've learned . . .', Marta Zaraska, in conversation with me on the *Power Hour* podcast, 16 June 2020.

p. 185 'You need humility . . .', 'Grant explains that . . .', Adam Grant, 'The best teams have this secret weapon', TED Talk, 31 May 2018.

p. 188 'If you get your . . .', Steve Sims, 'What You Need to Finally Make It Happen with Steve Sims', interview on *The Science of Success* podcast, 2 July 2020.

p. 192 'We don't like . . .', Aicha McKenzie, in conversation with me on the *Power Hour* podcast, 19 March 2019.

p. 193 'Remember that . . .', Ibid.

p. 199 'The book outlines . . .', Susan Cain, *Quiet: The Power of Introverts in a World That Can't Stop Talking* (London: Penguin Books, 2013).

p. 200 'He says that . . .', Jordan Harbinger, '6 Minute Networking', online course available on www.courses.jordanharbinger.com.

p. 201 'Imagine that you . . .', Ben Wharfe, in conversation with me on the *Power Hour* podcast, 27 August 2019.

p. 202 'One of the . . .', Ibid.

p. 205 'When a person . . .', Robert Frank, 'How self-made are today's billionaires?', *CNBC*, 3 October 2014.

The Power of Purpose

p. 220 'possibly the best . . .', *Athletics Weekly*, quoted on www.morgan-lake.com/morgan/.

p. 221 'It was quite . . .', Morgan Lake, in conversation with me on the *Power Hour* podcast, 2 July 2019.

p. 227 'podcast interview with . . .', Jesse Itzler, '#1127 – Jesse Itzler', interview on *The Joe Rogan Experience* podcast, 5 June 2018.

p. 234 'I was working . . .', IN-Q, 'Home', *Inquire Within* (New York: HarperOne, 2020).

p. 241 'I never advise . . .', Samantha Clarke, in conversation with me on the *Power Hour* podcast, 18 February 2020.

p. 242 'It might be that . . .', Ibid.

p. 243 'Author and motivational . . .', Simon Sinek, 'How great leaders inspire action', TED Talk, 4 May 2010.

p. 243 'one of the most . . .', Arianna Huffington quoted in Helen Booth, 'CV advice: the four skills you should always include, according to top CEOs', *Stylist Online*, 18 February 2020.

p. 246 'addicted to busy', Jody Shield, in conversation with me on the *Power Hour* podcast, 27 November 2018.

p. 247 'When we step . . .', Ibid.

p. 253 'Whenever the younger . . .', Trevor Nelson, in conversation with me on the *Power Hour* podcast, 15 October 2019.

Create Your Own Power Hour

p. 266 'This innovative concept . . .', Sir Dave Brailsford, in an interview with Eben Harrell, 'How 1% Performance Improvements Led to Olympic Gold', *Harvard Business Review*, 30 October 2015.

p. 270 'Scientist and author Cal . . .', 'ditch the tech', 'embrace the boredom', 'you'll become much . . .', Cal Newport, *Deep Work: Rules for Focused Success in a Distracted World* (London: Piatkus, 2016).

p. 271 'Countless studies have . . .', Lisa Quast, 'Want to Be More Productive? Stop Multi-tasking', *Forbes Magazine*, 6 February 2017.

p. 282 'According to psychologist . . .', 'One thing that is . . .', 'She defines self-awareness . . .', Dr Tasha Eurich, 'You Aren't Actually Self-Aware with Tasha Eurich', interview on *The Science of Success* podcast, 21 May 2020.

p. 284 'Dr Eurich's research concludes . . .', Ibid.